Made in China.

Not for individual sale.

Item #7600 Guest Book

Acquistition and Content Development—Peg Couch, Better Day Books;
Graphic Design—Michael Douglas; Technical Edit—Mary Sullivan Hutcheson.

HERE
WE COME
A-Caroling

Made in China.

Not for individual sale.

Item #7604 Guest Book

Acquistition and Content Development—Peg Couch, Better Day Books; Graphic Design—Michael Douglas; Technical Edit—Mary Sullivan Hutcheson.

HERE WE COME *A-Caroling*

Made in China.

Not for individual sale.

Item #7603 Guest Book

Acquistition and Content Development—Peg Couch, Better Day Books; Graphic Design—Michael Douglas; Technical Edit—Mary Sullivan Hutcheson.

JINGLE
Bells

Made in China.

Not for individual sale.

Item #7602 Guest Book

Acquistition and Content Development—Peg Couch, Better Day Books;
Graphic Design—Michael Douglas; Technical Edit—Mary Sullivan Hutcheson.

JINGLE Bells

THE
First Noel

WE Three Kings

Christmas Carol Songbook

25 FAVORITE SONGS
TO CELEBRATE THE MOST
WONDERFUL TIME
OF THE YEAR!

LEISURE ARTS, INC. • Maumelle, Arkansas

Made in China.

Not for individual sale.

Item #7601 Guest Book

Acquistition and Content Development—Peg Couch, Better Day Books; Graphic Design—Michael Douglas; Technical Edit—Mary Sullivan Hutcheson.

CONTENTS

INTRODUCTION

On the following pages, you'll find lyrics to twenty-five classic holiday songs. From *Deck the Halls* and *Silent Night* to *Jingle Bells*—there's something for all ages. Of course, there are many songs that you may know the chorus to, but having the lyrics to all of the verses comes in quite handy. You might even sing a little louder with the confidence of a book in your hand (and something to hide behind if you are shy).

The songs are numbered for your convenience. You can plan the order ahead of time or appoint a leader to call out the song number as you go. If you are traveling in the neighborhood, be sure all carolers have arrived at the door before ringing the doorbell.

LET THE
Merry-Making
BEGIN!

ANGELS WE HAVE HEARD ON HIGH

1

Angels we have heard on high
Sweetly singing o'er the plains
And the mountains in reply
Echoing their joyous strains
Gloria, in excelsis Deo!
Gloria, in excelsis Deo!

Shepherds, why this jubilee?
Why your joyous strains prolong?
What the gladsome tidings be?
Which inspire your heavenly songs?
Gloria, in excelsis Deo!
Gloria, in excelsis Deo!

Come to Bethlehem and see
Him whose birth the angels sing;
Come, adore on bended knee,
Christ the Lord, the newborn King.
Gloria, in excelsis Deo!
Gloria, in excelsis Deo!

See Him in a manger laid,
Jesus, Lord of heaven and earth;
Mary, Joseph, lend your aid,
With us sing our Savior's birth.
Gloria, in excelsis Deo!
Gloria, in excelsis Deo!

AULD Lang Syne

2

Should old acquaintance be forgot,
and never brought to mind?
Should old acquaintance be forgot,
and old lang syne?

CHORUS:
For auld lang syne, my dear,
for auld lang syne,
we'll take a cup of kindness yet,
for auld lang syne.

And surely you'll buy your pint cup!
and surely I'll buy mine!
And we'll take a cup o' kindness yet,
for auld lang syne.
(repeat chorus)

We two have run about the slopes,
and picked the daisies fine;
But we've wandered many a weary foot,
since auld lang syne.
(repeat chorus)

We two have paddled in the stream,
from morning sun till dine;
But seas between us broad have roared
since auld lang syne.
(repeat chorus)

And there's a hand my trusty friend!
And give me a hand o' thine!
And we'll take a right good-will draught,
for auld lang syne.
(repeat chorus)

Away In A Manger

3

Away in a manger, no crib for a bed,
The little Lord Jesus lay down his sweet head.
The stars in the bright sky looked down where he lay,
The little Lord Jesus asleep on the hay.

The cattle are lowing, the baby awakes,
But little Lord Jesus, no crying he makes.
I love thee, Lord Jesus! look down from the sky,
And stay by my cradle till morning is nigh.

Be near me, Lord Jesus; I ask thee to stay
Close by me forever, and love me I pray.
Bless all the dear children in thy tender care,
And take us to heaven to live with thee there.

DECK THE HALLS

4

Deck the halls with boughs of holly,
Fa, la, la, la, la, la, la, la, la!
'Tis the season to be jolly,
Fa, la, la, la, la, la, la, la, la!
Don we now our gay apparel,
Fa, la, la, la, la, la, la, la!
Troll the ancient Yule-tide carol,
Fa, la, la, la, la, la, la, la!

See the blazing yule before us,
Fa, la, la, la, la, la, la, la, la!
Strike the harp and join the chorus.
Fa, la, la, la, la, la, la, la, la!
Follow me in merry measure,
Fa, la, la, la, la, la, la, la!
While I tell of Yule-tide treasure,
Fa, la, la, la, la, la, la, la, la!

Fast away the old year passes,
Fa, la, la, la, la, la, la, la, la!
Hail the new, ye lads and lasses!
Fa, la, la, la, la, la, la, la, la!
Sing we joyous all together,
Fa, la, la, la, la, la, la, la!
Heedless of the wind and weather,
Fa, la, la, la, la, la, la, la, la!

DING DONG *Merrily* ON HIGH

5

Ding dong merrily on high,
In heav'n the bells are ringing:
Ding dong! verily the sky
Is riv'n with angel singing
Gloria Hosanna in excelsis!
Gloria Hosanna in excelsis!

E'en so here below, below,
Let steeple bells be swungen,
And "Io, io, io!"
By priest and people sungen
Gloria Hosanna in excelsis!
Gloria Hosanna in excelsis!

Pray you, dutifully prime
Your matin chime, ye ringers,
May you beautifully rhyme
Your eve'time song, ye singers
Gloria Hosanna in excelsis!
Gloria Hosanna in excelsis!

Gloria Hosanna in excelsis!
Gloria Hosanna in excelsis!
Hosanna in excelsis!!!

Good King Wenceslas

6

Good King Wenceslas looked out, on the Feast of Stephen,
When the snow lay round about, deep and crisp and even;
Brightly shone the moon that night, tho' the frost was cruel,
When a poor man came in sight, gath'ring winter fuel.

"Hither, page, and stand by me, if thou know'st it, telling,
Yonder peasant, who is he? Where and what his dwelling?"
"Sire, he lives a good league hence, underneath the mountain;
Right against the forest fence, by Saint Agnes' fountain."

"Bring me flesh, and bring me wine, bring me pine logs hither:
Thou and I shall see him dine, when we bear them thither."
Page and monarch, forth they went, forth they went together;
Through the rude wind's wild lament and the bitter weather.

"Sire, the night is darker now, and the wind blows stronger;
Fails my heart, I know not how; I can go no longer."
"Mark my footsteps, good my page. Tread thou in them boldly
Thou shalt find the winter's rage freeze thy blood less coldly."

In his master's steps he trod, where the snow lay dinted;
Heat was in the very sod which the saint had printed.
Therefore, Christian men, be sure, wealth or rank possessing,
Ye who now will bless the poor, shall yourselves find blessing.

HARK! THE HERALD ANGELS SING

7

Hark! The herald angels sing
"Glory to the newborn king;
Peace on earth and mercy mild,
God and sinners reconciled"
Joyful all ye nations rise,
Join the triumph of the skies
With the angelic host proclaim
"Christ is born in Bethlehem"
Hark! The herald-angels sing
"Glory to the newborn king"

Christ, by highest heaven adored
Christ, the everlasting Lord,
Late in time behold Him come
Offspring of a Virgin's womb:
Veiled in flesh the Godhead see,
Hail the incarnate Deity
Pleased as man with man to dwell
Jesus, our Emmanuel
Hark! The herald-angels sing
"Glory to the newborn king"

Hail the Heaven-born Prince of Peace!
Hail the Son of Righteousness!
Light and life to all He brings,
Risen with healing in His wings;
Mild He lays His glory by
Born that man no more may die
Born to raise the sons of earth
Born to give them second birth
Hark! The herald-angels sing
"Glory to the newborn king"

HERE
WE COME
A-Caroling

8

Here we come a-caroling
Among the leaves so green,
Here we come a wand'ring,
So fair to be seen.

CHORUS:
Love and joy come to you,
And to you glad Christmas too
And God bless you and send you a Happy New Year,
And God send you a Happy New Year.

We are not daily beggars
Who beg from door to door,
But we are friendly neighbors
Whom you have seen before.
(repeat chorus)

God bless the Master of this house,
Likewise the Mistress too
And all the little children,
That round the table go.
(repeat chorus)

I Heard The Bells On Christmas Day

9

I heard the bells on Christmas Day
Their old, familiar carols play,
and wild and sweet
The words repeat
Of peace on earth, good will to men!

I thought how as the day had come
The belfries of all Christendom
Had roll'd along
th' unbroken song
Of peace on earth, good will to men!

And in despair I bowed my head;
"There is no peace on earth," I said;
"For hate is strong,
And mocks the song
Of peace on earth, good will to men!"

Then pealed the bells more loud and deep:
"God is not dead, nor doth He sleep;
The wrong shall fail,
The right prevail,
With peace on earth, good will to men."

IT CAME UPON A MIDNIGHT CLEAR

10

It came upon a midnight clear,
That glorious song of old,
From angels bending near the earth,
To touch their harps of gold:
"Peace on the earth, goodwill to men,
From heaven's all-gracious King."
The world in solemn stillness lay,
To hear the angels sing.

Still through the cloven skies they come,
With peaceful wings unfurled,
And still their heavenly music floats
O'er all the weary world;
Above its sad and lowly plains,
They bend on hovering wing,
And ever o'er its babel sounds
The blessed angels sing.

Yet with the woes of sin and strife
The world has suffered long;
Beneath the angel-strain have rolled
Two thousand years of wrong;
And man, at war with man, hears not
The love-song which they bring;
O hush the noise, ye men of strife,
And hear the angels sing.

And ye, beneath life's crushing load,
Whose forms are bending low,
Who toil along the climbing way
With painful steps and slow,
Look now! for glad and golden hours
come swiftly on the wing.
O rest beside the weary road,
And hear the angels sing!

For lo!, the days are hastening on,
By prophet bards foretold,
When with the ever-circling years
Comes round the age of gold
When peace shall over all the earth
Its ancient splendors fling,
And the whole world give back the song
Which now the angels sing.

JINGLE
Bells

11

Dashing through the snow
In a one-horse open sleigh
O'er the fields we go
Laughing all the way

Bells on bob tail ring
Making spirits bright
What fun it is to ride and sing
A sleighing song tonight!

CHORUS:
Jingle bells, jingle bells,
Jingle all the way.
Oh! what fun it is to ride
In a one-horse open sleigh.
Jingle bells, jingle bells,
Jingle all the way;
Oh! what fun it is to ride
In a one-horse open sleigh.

A day or two ago
I thought I'd take a ride
And soon, Miss Fanny Bright
Was seated by my side,
The horse was lean and lank
Misfortune seemed his lot
He got into a drifted bank
And then we got upsot.
(repeat chorus)

A day or two ago,
The story I must tell
I went out on the snow,
And on my back I fell;
A gent was riding by
In a one-horse open sleigh,
He laughed as there I sprawling lie,
But quickly drove away.
(repeat chorus)

Now the ground is white
Go it while you're young,
Take the girls tonight
and sing this sleighing song;
Just get a bobtailed bay
Two forty as his speed
Hitch him to an open sleigh
And crack! you'll take the lead.
(repeat chorus)

Jolly Old Saint Nicholas

12

Jolly old Saint Nicholas
Lean your ear this way;
Don't you tell a single soul
What I'm going to say,
Christmas Eve is coming soon;
Now you dear old man,
Whisper what you'll bring to me;
Tell me if you can.

When the clock is striking twelve,
When I'm fast asleep,
Down the chimney broad and black
With your pack you'll creep;
All the stockings you will find
Hanging in a row;
Mine will be the shortest one;
You'll be sure to know.

Johnny wants a pair of skates;
Suzy wants a sled.
Nellie wants a picture book,
Yellow, blue and red.
Now I think I'll leave to you
What to give the rest.
Choose for me, dear Santa Claus,
You will know best.

JOY TO THE WORLD

13

Joy to the World; the Lord is come!
Let earth receive her King!
Let ev'ry heart prepare Him room,
And Heaven and nature sing.
And Heaven and nature sing.
And Heaven and nature sing.

Joy to the earth, the Savior reigns!
Let men their songs employ;
While fields & floods, rocks, hills & plains
Repeat the sounding joy.
Repeat the sounding joy.
Repeat the sounding joy.

No more let sins and sorrows grow,
Nor thorns infest the ground;
He comes to make his blessings flow
Far as the curse is found.
Far as the curse is found.
Far as the curse is found.

He rules the world with truth and grace,
And makes the nations prove
The glories of His righteousness,
And wonders of His love.
And wonders of His love.
And wonders of His love.

O Christmas TREE

14

O Christmas tree, O Christmas tree!
How lovely are thy branches!
O Christmas tree, O Christmas tree,
How lovely are thy branches!

Not only green when summer's here,
But in the coldest time of year.
O Christmas tree, O Christmas tree,
How lovely are thy branches!

O Christmas tree, O Christmas tree,
Much pleasure doth thou bring me!
O Christmas tree, O Christmas tree,
Much pleasure doth thou bring me!

For every year the Christmas tree,
Brings to us all both joy and glee.
O Christmas tree, O Christmas tree,
Much pleasure doth thou bring me!

O Christmas tree, O Christmas tree,
How sturdy God hath made thee!
O Christmas tree, O Christmas tree,
How sturdy God hath made thee!

Thou bidd'st us all place faithfully
Our trust in God, unchangingly!
O Christmas tree, O Christmas tree,
How sturdy God hath made thee!

O Christmas tree, O Christmas tree,
Thy candles shine out brightly!
O Christmas tree, O Christmas tree,
Thy candles shine out brightly!

Each bough doth hold its tiny light,
That makes each toy to sparkle bright.
O Christmas tree, O Christmas tree,
Thy candles shine out brightly!

O Come, All Ye Faithful

15

O come, all ye faithful, joyful and triumphant!
O come ye, O come ye to Bethlehem;
Come and behold him
Born the King of Angels:
O come, let us adore Him,
O come, let us adore Him,
O come, let us adore Him,
Christ the Lord.

God of God, light of light,
Lo, he abhors not the Virgin's womb;
True God, begotten, not created:
O come, let us adore Him,
O come, let us adore Him,
O come, let us adore Him,
Christ the Lord.

Sing, choirs of angels, sing in exultation,
Sing, all ye citizens of Heaven above!
Glory to God, glory in the highest:
O come, let us adore Him,
O come, let us adore Him,
O come, let us adore Him,
Christ the Lord.

Yea, Lord, we greet thee, born this happy morning;
Jesus, to thee be glory given!
Word of the Father, now in flesh appearing!
O come, let us adore Him,
O come, let us adore Him,
O come, let us adore Him,
Christ the Lord.

O COME, O COME, EMMANUEL

16

O come, O come, Emmanuel,
And ransom captive Israel,
That mourns in lonely exile here,
Until the Son of God appear.
Rejoice! Rejoice! Emmanuel
Shall come to thee, O Israel.

O come, Thou Rod of Jesse, free
Thine own from Satan's tyranny;
From depths of hell Thy people save,
And give them victory o'er the grave.
Rejoice! Rejoice! Emmanuel
Shall come to thee, O Israel.

O come, Thou Dayspring, from on high,
And cheer us by Thy drawing nigh;
Disperse the gloomy clouds of night,
And death's dark shadows put to flight.
Rejoice! Rejoice! Emmanuel
Shall come to thee, O Israel.

O come, Thou Key of David, come
And open wide our heav'nly home;
Make safe the way that leads on high,
And close the path to misery.
Rejoice! Rejoice! Emmanuel
Shall come to thee, O Israel.

O come, Adonai, Lord of might,
Who to Thy tribes, on Sinai's height,
In ancient times didst give the law
In cloud and majesty and awe.
Rejoice! Rejoice! Emmanuel
Shall come to thee, O Israel.

O Holy Night

17

O holy night! The stars are brightly shining,
It is the night of our dear Savior's birth.
Long lay the world in sin and error pining,
Till He appear'd and the soul felt its worth.
A thrill of hope, the weary world rejoices,
For yonder breaks a new and glorious morn.

Fall on your knees! O hear the angel voices!
O night divine, O night when Christ was born;
O night divine, O night, O night Divine.

Led by the light of Faith serenely beaming,
With glowing hearts by His cradle we stand.
So led by light of a star sweetly gleaming,
Here come the wise men from the Orient land.
The King of Kings lay thus in lowly manger;
In all our trials born to be our friend.

He knows our need, to our weaknesses no stranger,
Behold your King! Before Him lowly bend!
Behold your King, Before Him lowly bend!

Truly He taught us to love one another;
His law is love and His gospel is peace.
Chains shall He break for the slave is our brother;
And in His name all oppression shall cease.
Sweet hymns of joy in grateful chorus raise we,
Let all within us praise His holy name.

Christ is the Lord! O praise His Name forever,
His power and glory evermore proclaim.
His power and glory evermore proclaim.

O Little Town of Bethlehem

18

O little town of Bethlehem,
How still we see thee lie!
Above thy deep and dreamless sleep
The silent stars go by;
Yet in thy dark streets shineth
The everlasting Light;
The hopes and fears of all the years
Are met in thee tonight.

For Christ is born of Mary,
And gathered all above,
While mortals sleep, the angels keep
Their watch of wondering love.
O morning stars, together
Proclaim the holy birth!
And praises sing to God the King,
And peace to men on earth.

How silently, how silently,
The wondrous gift is given!
So God imparts to human hearts
The blessings of his heaven.
No ear may hear his coming,
But in this world of sin,
Where meek souls will receive him, still
The dear Christ enters in.

Where children pure and happy
Pray to the blessed Child,
Where misery cries out to thee,
Son of the mother mild;
Where charity stands watching
And faith holds wide the door,
The dark night wakes, the glory breaks,
And Christmas comes once more.

O holy Child of Bethlehem!
Descend to us, we pray;
Cast out our sin and enter in,
Be born in us today.
We hear the Christmas angels
The great glad tidings tell;
O come to us, abide with us,
Our Lord Emmanuel!

SILENT NIGHT

19

Silent night, holy night,
All is calm, all is bright
Round yon virgin mother and child.
Holy infant, so tender and mild,
Sleep in heavenly peace,
Sleep in heavenly peace.

Silent night, holy night,
Shepherds quake at the sight;
Glories stream from heaven afar,
Heavenly hosts sing Alleluia!
Christ the Savior is born,
Christ the Savior is born!

Silent night, holy night,
Son of God, love's pure light;
Radiant beams from thy holy face
With the dawn of redeeming grace,
Jesus, Lord, at thy birth,
Jesus, Lord, at thy birth.

THE First Noel

20

The First Noel, the Angels did say
Was to certain poor shepherds in fields as they lay
In fields where they lay keeping their sheep
On a cold winter's night that was so deep.
Noel, Noel, Noel, Noel
Born is the King of Israel!

They looked up and saw a star
Shining in the East beyond them far
And to the earth it gave great light
And so it continued both day and night.
Noel, Noel, Noel, Noel
Born is the King of Israel!

And by the light of that same star
Three Wise men came from country far
To seek for a King was their intent
And to follow the star wherever it went.
Noel, Noel, Noel, Noel
Born is the King of Israel!

This star drew nigh to the northwest
O'er Bethlehem it took its rest
And there it did both pause and stay
Right o'er the place where Jesus lay.
Noel, Noel, Noel, Noel
Born is the King of Israel!

Then entered in those Wise men three
Fell reverently upon their knee
And offered there in His presence
Their gold and myrrh and frankincense.
Noel, Noel, Noel, Noel
Born is the King of Israel!

Then let us all with one accord
Sing praises to our heavenly Lord
That hath made Heaven and earth of nought
And with his blood mankind has bought.
Noel, Noel, Noel, Noel
Born is the King of Israel!

The Twelve Days of Christmas

21

On the first day of Christmas my true love sent to me
A partridge in a pear tree.

On the second day of Christmas my true love sent to me
Two turtle doves
And a partridge in a pear tree.

On the third day of Christmas my true love sent to me
Three French hens,
Two turtle doves,
And a partridge in a pear tree.

On the fourth day of Christmas my true love sent to me
Four calling birds,
Three French hens,
Two turtle doves,
And a partridge in a pear tree.

On the fifth day of Christmas my true love sent to me
Five gold rings
Four calling birds,
Three French hens,
Two turtle doves,
And a partridge in a pear tree.

(continued on next page)

On the sixth day of Christmas my true love sent to me
Six geese a-laying,
Five gold rings
Four calling birds,
Three French hens,
Two turtle doves,
And a partridge in a pear tree.

On the seventh day of Christmas my true love sent to me
Seven swans a-swimming,
Six geese a-laying,
Five gold rings
Four calling birds,
Three French hens,
Two turtle doves,
And a partridge in a pear tree.

On the eighth day of Christmas my true love sent to me
Eight maids a-milking,
Seven swans a-swimming,
Six geese a-laying,
Five gold rings
Four calling birds,
Three French hens,
Two turtle doves,
And a partridge in a pear tree.

On the ninth day of Christmas my true love sent to me
Nine ladies dancing,
Eight maids a-milking,
Seven swans a-swimming,
Six geese a-laying,
Five gold rings
Four calling birds,
Three French hens,
Two turtle doves,
And a partridge in a pear tree.

On the tenth day of Christmas my true love sent to me
Ten lords a-leaping,
Nine ladies dancing,
Eight maids a-milking,
Seven swans a-swimming,
Six geese a-laying,
Five gold rings
Four calling birds,
Three French hens,
Two turtle doves,
And a partridge in a pear tree.

On the eleventh day of Christmas my true love sent to me
Eleven pipers piping,
Ten lords a-leaping,
Nine ladies dancing,
Eight maids a-milking,
Seven swans a-swimming,
Six geese a-laying,
Five gold rings
Four calling birds,
Three French hens,
Two turtle doves,
And a partridge in a pear tree.

On the twelfth day of Christmas my true love sent to me
Twelve drummers drumming,
Eleven pipers piping,
Ten lords a-leaping,
Nine ladies dancing,
Eight maids a-milking,
Seven swans a-swimming,
Six geese a-laying,
Five gold rings
Four calling birds,
Three French hens,
Two turtle doves,
And a partridge in a pear tree.

UP ON THE HOUSETOP

22

Up on the housetop reindeer pause
Out jumps good old Santa Claus.
Down through the chimney, with lots of toys,
All for the little ones' Christmas joys.

CHORUS:
Ho, ho, ho! Who wouldn't go.
Ho, ho, ho! Who wouldn't go,
Up on the house top, click, click, click;
Down through the chimney with good Saint Nick.

First comes the stocking of little Nell;
Oh, dear Santa fill it well!
Give her a dolly that laughs and cries;
One that will open and shut her eyes.
(repeat chorus)

Next comes the stocking of little Will;
Oh just see what a glorious fill!
Here is a hammer and lots of tacks;
A whistle and a ball and a whip that cracks!
(repeat chorus)

WE
Three Kings

23

We Three Kings of Orient are,
Bearing gifts we traverse afar,
Field and fountain,
Moor and mountain,
Following yonder Star.

CHORUS:
O Star of Wonder, Star of Night,
Star with Royal Beauty bright,
Westward leading,
Still proceeding,
Guide us to Thy perfect Light.

Born a King on Bethlehem plain,
Gold I bring to crown Him again,
King for ever,
Ceasing never
Over us all to reign.
(repeat chorus)

Frankincense to offer have I,
Incense owns a Deity nigh:
Prayer and praising
All men raising,
Worship Him God on High.
(repeat chorus)

Myrrh is mine; its bitter perfume
Breathes a life of gathering gloom;
Sorrowing, sighing,
Bleeding, dying,
Sealed in the stone-cold tomb.
(repeat chorus)

Glorious now behold Him arise,
King, and God, and Sacrifice;
Heav'n sings Hallelujah:
Hallelujah the earth replies.
(repeat chorus)

We Wish
You A Merry
Christmas

24

We wish you a merry Christmas,
We wish you a merry Christmas,
We wish you a merry Christmas
And a happy New Year.
Good tidings we bring
To you and your kin;
We wish you a merry Christmas
And a happy New Year!

Oh, bring us some figgy pudding,
Oh, bring us some figgy pudding,
Oh, bring us some figgy pudding,
And bring it right here.
Good tidings we bring
To you and your kin;
We wish you a merry Christmas
And a happy New Year!

We won't go till we get some,
We won't go till we get some,
We won't go till we get some,
So bring it right here.
Good tidings we bring
To you and your kin;
We wish you a merry Christmas
And a happy New Year!

We all like our figgy pudding,
We all like our figgy pudding,
We all like our figgy pudding,
With all its good cheers
Good tidings we bring
To you and your kin
We wish you a merry Christmas
And a happy New Year.

WHAT CHILD IS THIS?

25

What child is this, who, laid to rest,
On Mary's lap is sleeping?
Whom angels greet with anthems sweet,
While shepherds watch are keeping?

This, this is Christ the King,
Whom shepherds guard and angels sing:
Haste, haste to bring him laud,
The babe, the son of Mary.

So bring him incense, gold, and myrrh,
Come, peasant, king, to own him.
the King of kings salvation brings,
Let loving hearts enthrone him.

Raise, raise the song on high!
While Mary sings a lullaby.
Joy, joy for Christ is born,
The Babe, the son of Mary.

Carolers

Name:..

Date:...

Favorite Holiday Songs: ....

....

....

....

Name:..

Date:...

Favorite Holiday Songs: ....

....

....

....

Name:..

Date:...

Favorite Holiday Songs: ....

....

....

....

Carolers

Name:

Date:

Favorite Holiday Songs:

Name:

Date:

Favorite Holiday Songs:

Name:

Date:

Favorite Holiday Songs:

Carolers

Name:..

Date:...

Favorite Holiday Songs: ....

....

....

....

Name:..

Date:...

Favorite Holiday Songs: ....

....

....

....

Name:..

Date:...

Favorite Holiday Songs: ....

....

....

....

Carolers

Name:

Date:

Favorite Holiday Songs:

Name:

Date:

Favorite Holiday Songs:

Name:

Date:

Favorite Holiday Songs:

MERRY
Christmas
TO ALL!

Christmas Carol Songbook

25 FAVORITE SONGS,
DELICIOUS HOLIDAY RECIPES,
PARTY IDEAS & MORE!

LEISURE ARTS, INC. • Maumelle, Arkansas

Made in China.

Not for individual sale.

Item #7599 Hostess Guide

Images used under license from CreativeMarket.com and Shutterstock.com.

Acquistition and Content Development—Peg Couch, Better Day Books;
Graphic Design—Michael Douglas; Technical Edit—Mary Sullivan Hutcheson.

May your
Heart be Merry,
your Season Bright
and your Home
Filled with Song this
Holiday Season!

CONTENTS

INTRODUCTION

Ready or not, the holidays are here again. And, if you're like many people you've promised yourself that this year will be different. No more last-minute shopping, overspending and running yourself ragged before the tinsel is on the tree. This year, you have committed to slow down, savor the season and truly enjoy the company of friends, family and neighbors. One of the many ways to reignite the magic of Christmas is to bring back the old traditions that so many of us are nostalgic for...like Christmas caroling.

With this keepsake set, you not only get 5 matching Christmas Carol Songbooks filled with 25 of the most popular holiday songs, but you also get this expanded Hostess Guide that includes great ideas for holiday entertaining, tips and tools for planning, 25 holiday cookie recipes, 25 great holiday party ideas and guest book pages for documenting memories.

We hope that you will pull these books out year after year with warm memories of bringing good cheer to all as your lift your voices in song.

Merry Christmas!

Ready,
Set,
Merry!

Entertaining Tips, Worksheets & Party Ideas

Looking for ways to spend more time enjoying the holidays and less time stressing over them? We've got you covered! In the coming pages, you will find tips, planning sheets and lots of fun party themes to celebrate the season. Whether you are hosting an all-out caroling party or looking for other fun event ideas to tie-in with caroling—you'll find something to suit your guests, your entertaining style and your budget.

Host A Caroling Party

The tree is up, the mistletoe is hung and the wreath is on the front door. It's time to host your Christmas Caroling party. Here are some tips to make sure it's a great event:

Pick A Date

Like all holiday events, you will want to plan early and before everyone's calendar is booked...the week or two before Christmas is usually best. Also, if you are caroling around the neighborhood, think about times when people might be home. Weekend evenings are a great choice. Finally, be mindful of the time. You don't want to arrive as people are sitting down to dinner...or in bed!

Invitations

Each of us has our own entertaining style. So, if you are on the more formal side, a printed invitation is always elegant. For more informal gatherings feel free to do an online posting or emailed invitation. Along with the obvious details of time, date, location—be sure to advise if you are caroling outside so that people can dress appropriately for the weather.

Create the Menu

When selecting menu items for your caroling party think about when your guests will be arriving and what time you plan to depart for caroling. The time between these two events will dictate what to serve. A good rule of thumb is to do snacks and appetizers before departing and dessert upon your return. If you are caroling at home or around a fire in the backyard—you can set a buffet ahead of time and allow for continuous grazing! A hot cocoa bar is always a fun idea to warm chilly carolers. Get creative and add candy cane stir sticks, whipped cream and red or green sprinkles. See the recipe section of this book for some great ideas.

Make it Cozy

Caroling is a fun event that evokes the warm spirit of the season. Add extra feelings of comfort with small touches. If you are caroling outside, place some blankets over the furniture so people can warm themselves. A woolen tartan blanket is a great choice, but use what you have! If you are caroling inside, light some holiday-scented candles or put a log on the fire. Don't be afraid to cuddle up as you sing because...baby, it's probably cold outside!

Plan for Music

This book includes the lyrics to 25 popular Christmas carols. Most people can sing these without having to follow sheet music. However, if you want some instrumental backdrop, ask a musical friend or family member to play the piano (if you have one) or create a playlist. Another really fun and festive idea is to break out those old vinyl Christmas albums...if you still have a way to play them!

Tips

- Be careful if you are caroling outside at night; walk on the sidewalks.
- Carry flashlights and dress for the weather.
- Plan your route ahead of time.
- Be courteous; don't walk on lawns or in gardens and flower beds.
- Leave pets at home; all the merry making may frighten your furry one.
- Be mindful of the time; avoid dinner and bedtime.
- Have a "the more the merrier" mindset; you'll be surprised how many carolers you might pick up along the way!

Eat, Drink and Be Merry!

25 Festive Party THEMES

1
COOKIE SWAP PARTY

2
HANGING O' THE GREENS PARTY

3
TREE TRIMMING PARTY

4
GIFT WRAPPING PARTY

5
MYSTERY GIFT EXCHANGE PARTY

6
JINGLE & MINGLE OPEN HOUSE PARTY

7
UGLY CHRISTMAS SWEATER PARTY

8
HOLIDAY CARD MAKING PARTY

9
ORNAMENT CRAFTING PARTY

10
VISIT FROM SANTA KIDS' PARTY

11
FAVORITE THINGS PARTY

12
DON'T BE A GRINCH PARTY

13
HOLIDAY WREATH MAKING PARTY

14
VERY MERRY PET PARTY

15
HOLIDAY MOVIE NIGHT PARTY

16
NAUGHTY OR NICE PARTY

17
PANCAKES & PJ'S HOLIDAY PARTY

18
HOT COCOA BAR PARTY

19
FESTIVE FLANNEL PARTY

20
GINGERBREAD DECORATING PARTY

21
AROUND THE WORLD HOLIDAY PARTY

22
WINTER WONDERLAND PARTY

23
COOKIE DECORATING PARTY

24
HOLIDAY BRUNCH BUFFET

25
GIVE BACK HOLIDAY PARTY

Holiday Party Planning

Guest List:

....
....
....
....
....
....
....
....
....
....
....
....
....
....
....
....
....
....
....
....
....

Date:

....

Time:

....

Location:

....

RSVP:

....

Send Invites by:

....

Decorating completed by:

....

Shopping completed by:

....

Notes:

....
....
....
....
....

Menu

Snacks/Appetizers:

....

....

....

....

....

Mains:

....

....

....

....

....

....

Desserts:

....

....

....

....

Beverages:

....

....

....

Shopping List:

....

....

....

....

....

....

....

....

....

....

....

....

....

....

....

Specialty Store:

....

....

....

....

....

Holiday Party Planning

Guest List:

....
....
....
....
....
....
....
....
....
....
....
....
....
....
....
....
....
....
....
....

Date:

....

Time:

....

Location:

....

RSVP:

....

Send Invites by:

....

Decorating completed by:

....

Shopping completed by:

....

Notes:

....
....
....
....
....

Menu

Snacks/Appetizers:

Mains:

Desserts:

Beverages:

Shopping List:

Specialty Store:

Holiday Party Planning

Guest List:

....
....
....
....
....
....
....
....
....
....
....
....
....
....
....
....
....
....
....
....
....

Date:

....

Time:

....

Location:

....

RSVP:

....

Send Invites by:

....

Decorating completed by:

....

Shopping completed by:

....

Notes:

....
....
....
....
....

Menu

Snacks/Appetizers:

Mains:

Desserts:

Beverages:

Shopping List:

Specialty Store:

Recipes

Appetizers, Giftable Snacks, Cookies and Hot Beverages

It's the most wonderful time of the year! And, for many of us that means trimming the tree, long shopping trips, watching classic holiday movies, wrapping presents and cooking—lots of cooking! Whether you are hosting a caroling party at your home or creating edible gifts for neighbors, the following pages will provide you with creative recipes that are both inexpensive and easy to prepare. So, put on your red apron, turn up the holiday tunes, and let's get cooking...it's Christmas!

Artichoke & Roasted Red Pepper Dip

2 large sweet red peppers
1/4 cup sliced green onions
2 tablespoons butter or margarine
1 can (14 oz) artichoke hearts, drained and chopped
1-1/4 cups freshly grated Parmesan cheese, divided
1 cup mayonnaise
1/2 cup sour cream
1/4 teaspoon salt
1/8 teaspoon ground red pepper
Green onion to garnish
Crackers to serve

To roast sweet red peppers, cut in half lengthwise and remove seeds and membranes. Place, skin side up, on an ungreased baking sheet; flatten peppers with hand. Broil about 3 inches from heat about 10 minutes or until peppers are blackened. Immediately seal peppers in a plastic bag and allow to steam 10 to 15 minutes. Remove and discard charred skin; coarsely chop peppers. Lower oven temperature to 350 degrees.

In a medium skillet over medium heat, cook 1/4 cup green onions in butter until tender. Remove from heat. Stir in artichoke hearts, 1 cup Parmesan cheese, mayonnaise, sour cream, salt, ground red pepper and roasted peppers. Transfer to 3 greased 1-1/4-cup ramekins. Garnish with remaining 1/4 cup Parmesan cheese and green onion. Bake uncovered dip 15 minutes or until heated through. Serve warm with crackers or bread.

YIELD: about 3-1/4 cups dip

Baked Crab Dip

- 1 package (8 oz) cream cheese, softened
- 1/2 cup mayonnaise
- 2 tablespoons freshly squeezed lemon juice
- 1 tablespoon grated onion
- 1 tablespoon prepared horseradish
- 1/4 teaspoon garlic salt
- 1/4 teaspoon ground white pepper
- 1/8 teaspoon hot pepper sauce
- 8 oz fresh crabmeat or 2 cans crabmeat (6 oz each), drained
- 1/4 cup finely chopped water chestnuts

Preheat oven to 350 degrees. In a large bowl, beat cream cheese, mayonnaise, lemon juice, onion, horseradish, garlic salt, white pepper and pepper sauce until well blended. Fold in crabmeat and water chestnuts. Spoon into a 3-cup baking dish. Bake 15 to 20 minutes or until lightly browned around edges. Serve warm with crackers.

YIELD: about 2-1/2 cups dip

HOLIDAY TRIVIA!

How many reindeer pull Santa's sleigh?

— ANSWER FOUND ON PAGE 127 —

All Hail, The Holiday Cheese Board!

If you are looking for a show-stopping appetizer that is inexpensive, easy-to-prepare and always delicious—look no further than the crowd-pleasing cheeseboard. Made from store-bought ingredients, this is the busy host's or hostess' secret weapon. All you need is a large kitchen board (wood, slate or even marble) and a variety of cheeses, bread or crackers and fruits (dried and fresh). From there, you can build more elaborate cheese boards using any number of ingredients such as cured meats, savory spreads, sweet jams, spiced nuts and fresh vegetables. The ideas are endless and it literally takes minutes (not hours!) to prepare.

GET CREATIVE!

Add a festive flair by garnishing your cheese board with fresh rosemary and cranberries.

Cheeses

Variety is key when selecting the cheeses. Be sure to add various textures (both hard and soft) as well as a range of tastes from sharp to mellow. You can plan approximately one or two ounces per person and serve at room temperature. Use both yellow and white cheeses to add additional variety to your board.

Kinds of Cheeses

- **Soft:** Brie, Fresh Mozzarella, Goat
- **Semi-Soft:** Fontina, Gouda, Jarlesberg, Stilton
- **Semi-Hard:** Gruyere, Manchego, Provolone
- **Hard:** Aged Asiago, Aged Cheddar, Parmesan

Additional Accoutrements

Here are some ideas for ingredients to add color, texture and flavor to your cheese board. There are no rules here, so customize to suit your tastes and that of your guests. Check local shops and farm or specialty markets for great selections. Don't be afraid to ask the purveyor for advice on beverage pairings and more.

Breads and Crackers

- Sliced baguette, ciabatta, bread sticks
- Multigrain crackers, poppy seed crackers, buttery crackers
- Bagel chips and crisps

Sweet Ingredients

- Fig preserves, orange marmalade, local honey
- Dried apricots, dried cranberry, dried pineapple
- Fresh fruit: Grapes, blackberries, cantaloupe, pear

Savory Ingredients

- Meats (charcuterie): Hard salami, dry-cured chorizo, prosciutto
- Nuts: Almonds, pistachios, macadamia nuts
- Olives: Black, green, tapenade

Putting it All Together

You want a board that is full, plentiful and colorful. Arrange your crackers or bread in rows on either side of the platter. Place your cheeses around the platter with room in between each offering. Fill the spaces between the cheese with other items such as nuts, dried fruits and meats. Place jams, jellies or spreads in small cups and add them to the platter, each with a small spreader. Slice or cube cheeses in advance and be sure to arrange small plates and cocktail napkins next to the platter for your guests' convenience. *Enjoy!*

Bruschetta

3 large cloves garlic, minced
2 tablespoons olive oil, plus more for brushing bread
4 cups peeled, seeded and chopped Roma tomatoes (about 2-1/4 pounds)
2 tablespoons balsamic vinegar
2 tablespoons chopped fresh basil leaves
1/2 teaspoon ground black pepper
1/2 teaspoon salt
1 baguette French bread (10 ounces and about 2-1/2 inches in diameter)

In a large saucepan, sauté garlic in 2 tablespoons olive oil over medium heat about 2 minutes or until garlic begins to brown. Stir in tomatoes and vinegar. Stirring frequently, cook about 20 minutes or until mixture thickens and volume reduces by half. Stir in basil, pepper and salt.

Cut bread into 1/2-inch-thick slices. Toast bread slices under broiler about 1 minute on each side. Brush top of each slice with olive oil. Place 1-1/2 to 2 teaspoons topping on each slice; broil about 3 minutes or until heated through. Serve immediately.

YIELD: about 38 appetizers

Herb Cheese Spread

1 package (8 oz) cream cheese, softened
1/4 cup butter or margarine, softened
1-1/2 tablespoons milk
1/4 teaspoon garlic powder
1/4 teaspoon ground savory
1/8 teaspoon ground oregano
1/8 teaspoon dried dill weed
1/8 teaspoon dried basil leaves
1/8 teaspoon ground black pepper

In a small bowl, beat all ingredients with an electric mixer until well blended. Store in an airtight container in refrigerator. Serve with crackers.

YIELD: about 1-1/3 cups spread

HOLIDAY TRIVIA!

How many times is figgy pudding demanded in the song, "We Wish You a Merry Christmas"?

— ANSWER FOUND ON PAGE 127 —

Tomato-Basil-Walnut Brie

1 can (6 oz) tomato paste
2 tablespoons firmly packed brown sugar
2 tablespoons chopped fresh basil leaves
1/2 cup finely chopped walnuts, toasted
1 package (8 oz) round Brie cheese
8 large whole fresh basil leaves

Preheat oven to 350 degrees. In a small bowl, combine tomato paste, brown sugar and chopped basil leaves; stir until well blended. Stir in walnuts. Place whole basil leaves in a circle in a round 2-cup oven-proof dish. Slice off top one-third of cheese. Place bottom two-thirds of cheese on leaves. Spoon about 1/2 cup tomato mixture onto cheese. Top with remaining piece of cheese. Spread remaining tomato mixture over top of cheese. Fold basil leaves over tomato mixture. Bake for 25 minutes or until cheese melts. Serve warm.

YIELD: 2 cups spread

Slow Cooker Reuben Dip

1 jar (16 oz) sauerkraut, drained
3 cups shredded Swiss cheese
1 package (8 oz) cream cheese
3/4 pound deli corned beef, cut into small pieces
3/4 cup Thousand Island dressing
Toasted party rye cocktail bread to serve

Combine sauerkraut, cream cheese, Swiss cheese, corned beef and dressing in slow cooker. Cover and cook on Low for 2 hours or until mixture is hot and cheese is melted, stirring occasionally. Serve with rye cocktail bread.

YIELD: about 4 cups dip

HOLIDAY TRIVIA!

What two reindeer names start with the letter "C"?

— ANSWER FOUND ON PAGE 127 —

Barbecued Peanuts

1/4 cup Worcestershire sauce
3 tablespoons vegetable oil
1/2 cup plus 6 tablespoons firmly packed brown sugar, divided
1-1/2 teaspoons dried minced onion
1 teaspoon apple cider vinegar
1 teaspoon hot pepper sauce
1 teaspoon garlic powder
1/4 teaspoon ground red pepper
2 containers (12 ounces each) lightly salted peanuts

Preheat oven to 250 degrees. In a heavy large skillet, combine Worcestershire sauce and oil. Stir in 1/2 cup brown sugar, onion, vinegar, pepper sauce, garlic powder and red pepper. Stirring frequently, cook over medium heat about 3 minutes or until sugar dissolves. Remove from heat. Add peanuts; stir until well coated. Spread peanut mixture on a jellyroll pan. Bake 1 hour, stirring every 10 minutes. Sprinkle remaining 6 tablespoons brown sugar over hot peanuts; toss until coated. Spread on lightly greased aluminum foil to cool. Store in an airtight container.

YIELD: about 7 cups peanuts

Cinnamon-Praline Pecans

1 egg white
1/2 cup firmly packed brown sugar
1 tablespoon praline liqueur
1 teaspoon ground cinnamon
1/2 teaspoon vanilla extract
1/2 teaspoon butter extract
1/8 teaspoon salt
2 cups pecan halves

Preheat oven to 225 degrees. In a medium bowl, beat egg white until soft peaks form. Fold in brown sugar, liqueur, cinnamon, extracts and salt. Fold in pecans. Bake 1 hour in a single layer on a greased nonstick jellyroll pan. Spread on aluminum foil to cool. Store in an airtight container.

YIELD: about 4 cups pecans

HOLIDAY TRIVIA!

In the song, "The 12 Days of Christmas", what is given on the 9th day?

— ANSWER FOUND ON PAGE 127 —

Sweet & Spicy Nuts

1 tablespoon sugar
1/2 teaspoon ground cumin
1/2 teaspoon chili powder
1/4 teaspoon ground red pepper
1/8 teaspoon salt
1 can (12 oz) mixed nuts

Preheat oven to 325 degrees. In a medium bowl, combine sugar, cumin, chili powder, red pepper and salt; set aside. Place nuts on a baking sheet. Bake 10 minutes. Toss warm nuts in spice mix until well coated. Transfer to baking sheet to cool. Store in an airtight container.

YIELD: about 2-1/2 cups nuts

HOLIDAY TRIVIA!

In what year was the first Christmas tree erected at Rockefeller Center in New York City?

— ANSWER FOUND ON PAGE 127 —

Cheesy Herb Crackers

2 packages (10 oz each) oyster crackers
1/2 cup vegetable oil
1/4 cup grated Parmesan cheese
1 package (1-1/4 oz) cheese sauce mix
3/4 teaspoon garlic powder
1/2 teaspoon ground oregano
1/2 teaspoon celery seed
1/2 teaspoon salt
1/8 teaspoon ground red pepper

Preheat oven to 300 degrees. Place oyster crackers in a large roasting pan. In a small bowl, combine oil, Parmesan cheese, cheese sauce mix, garlic powder, oregano, celery seed, salt and red pepper; whisk until blended. Pour oil mixture over crackers; stir until well coated. Place crackers on a baking sheet. Bake 15 minutes, stirring every 5 minutes. Spread on aluminum foil to cool. Store in an airtight container.

YIELD: about 12 cups snack mix

Christmas Cookie Countdown

25 Recipes to Sweeten the Holiday Season

What would the holidays be without a dash of sugar and the sweet smell of cookies baking in the oven? On the following pages, you will find plenty of delicious recipes for holiday treats. Whether you are baking with the kids, preparing for a cookie swap or making homemade goodies for friends and neighbors—you're sure to find the perfect holiday cookie. And, with 25 recipes to choose from... you'll be counting down the days to Christmas one cookie at a time!

1

Cherry Bit Cookies

- 1-1/4 cups butter or margarine, softened
- 2-1/4 cups sugar
- 2 eggs
- 1-1/2 teaspoons vanilla extract
- 1 teaspoon cherry flavoring
- 4-1/2 cups all-purpose flour
- 1 teaspoon baking powder
- 3/4 teaspoon salt
- 1 jar (10 oz) maraschino cherries, finely chopped and well drained

In a large bowl, cream butter and sugar until fluffy. Add eggs, vanilla and cherry flavoring; beat until smooth. In a medium bowl, combine flour, baking powder, and salt. Add dry ingredients to creamed mixture; stir until a soft dough forms. Stir in cherries. Divide dough into fourths and wrap in plastic wrap; chill two hours.

Preheat oven to 350 degrees. On a lightly floured surface, use a floured rolling pin to roll out one fourth of dough to 1/8-inch thickness. Use a 4-inch-wide heart-shaped cookie cutter to cut out cookies. Transfer to an ungreased baking sheet. Bake 8 to 10 minutes or until bottoms are lightly browned. Transfer cookies to a wire rack to cool. Repeat with remaining dough. Store in an airtight container.

YIELD: About 3-1/2 dozen cookies

2

Chocolate Coconut Shortbread Wedges

- 1-1/2 cups flaked coconut
- 1-1/2 cups slivered almonds, toasted
- 1 cup butter, softened
- 2/3 cup sugar
- 1-1/2 teaspoons vanilla extract
- 1-2/3 cups all-purpose flour
- 1/3 cup cocoa
- 1/2 teaspoon salt

Preheat oven to 350 degrees. Process coconut and almonds in a food processor until coarsely ground. In a medium bowl, cream butter and sugar until fluffy. Beat in vanilla. In a small bowl, combine flour, cocoa and salt. Gradually add dry ingredients; beat just until blended. Stir in coconut mixture.

Divide dough into thirds. Pat each third of dough into a 7-inch-diameter circle on a baking sheet lined with parchment paper. Bake 25 to 30 minutes or until firm. Transfer baking sheet to a wire rack; cool 10 minutes. Transfer shortbread on paper to a firm surface. Cut each warm shortbread into 8 wedges; cool completely. Store in an airtight container.

YIELD: 2 dozen shortbread wedges

3

Chocolate Gingersnaps

1-1/2 cups butter or margarine, softened
2-3/4 cups sugar, divided
2 eggs
1/2 cup molasses
4 cups all-purpose flour
1/4 cup plus 2 tablespoons cocoa, divided
2 teaspoons baking soda
2 teaspoons ground cinnamon
2 teaspoons ground cloves
2 teaspoons ground ginger

Preheat oven to 375 degrees. In a large bowl, cream butter and 2 cups of sugar until fluffy. Add eggs and molasses; beat until smooth. In a medium bowl, combine flour, 1/4 cup cocoa, baking soda, cinnamon, cloves and ginger. Add dry ingredients to creamed mixture; stir until a soft dough forms. In a small bowl, combine remaining 3/4 cup sugar and 2 tablespoons cocoa. Shape dough into 1-inch balls; roll in sugar mixture. Place balls 3 inches apart on a lightly greased baking sheet. Flatten balls into 2-inch diameter cookies with bottom of a glass dipped in sugar mixture. Bake 5 to 7 minutes or until bottoms are lightly browned. Transfer cookies to a wire rack to cool. Store in an airtight container.

YIELD: about 10 dozen cookies

4

Chocolate-Mint Sandwich Cookies

1-1/2 packages (12 oz each) round butter-flavored crackers

1 container (16 oz) chocolate ready-to-spread frosting

1 package (1 pound, 8 oz) chocolate candy coating, chopped

2 packages (10 oz each) mint chocolate chips

Place half of crackers (about 84 crackers) on wax paper. Spoon frosting into a pastry bag fitted with a large round tip. Pipe about 1 teaspoon of frosting onto each cracker. Place remaining crackers on top of frosting and press lightly.

In a heavy large saucepan, melt candy coating and chocolate chips over low heat. Remove from heat. Dip each cracker sandwich into chocolate. Please on wax paper and let chocolate harden. Store in an airtight container in a cool place.

YIELD: about 7 dozen cookies

5

Chocolate-Peanut Butter Cup Cookies

1 package (18 oz) refrigerated peanut butter cookie dough
1 bag (13 oz) mini peanut butter cups

Preheat oven to 350 degrees. Shape dough into 1-inch balls. Place balls in greased cups of a miniature muffin pan. Press a peanut butter cup into center of each ball. Bake 10 to 12 minutes or until edges are firm. Cool in pan 5 minutes. Remove from pan and cool completely on a wire rack. Store in an airtight container.

YIELD: About 3 dozen cookies

HOLIDAY TRIVIA!

What fabric was Frosty's hat made from?

— ANSWER FOUND ON PAGE 127 —

6

Christmas Button Cookies

- 1 cup butter or margarine, softened
- 3 oz cream cheese, softened
- 1 cup sugar
- 1 egg yolk
- 1 teaspoon almond extract
- 2-1/2 cups all-purpose flour
- 1 package (4 oz) red candied cherries
- 1 package (4 oz) green candied cherries

In a large bowl, cream butter, cream cheese and sugar until fluffy. Add egg yolk and almond extract; beat until smooth. Add flour to creamed mixture; stir until a soft dough forms. Wrap in plastic wrap and chill 1 hour.

Preheat oven to 325 degrees. Shape dough into 1-inch balls and place 2 inches apart on a greased baking sheet. Use thumb to make a slight indentation in top of each ball. Bake 12 to 15 minutes or until bottoms of cookies are lightly browned. Press a candied cherry into indentation in each warm cookie. Transfer cookies to a wire rack to cool. Store in an airtight container.

YIELD: about 5-1/2 dozen cookies

7

Cinnamon Cookies

COOKIES

- 1-1/2 cups vegetable shortening
- 3-1/2 cups sugar
- 2 eggs
- 1/2 cup water
- 1 teaspoon vanilla extract
- 5 cups all-purpose flour
- 1 tablespoon ground cinnamon
- 2 teaspoons baking powder
- 1 teaspoon salt

ICING

- 3/4 cup vegetable shortening
- 4-1/4 cups confectioners sugar
- 1 teaspoon vanilla extract
- 4–5 tablespoons milk

Preheat oven to 375°. For cookies, cream shortening and sugar in a large bowl until fluffy. Add eggs, water, and vanilla; beat until smooth. In a large bowl, combine flour, cinnamon, baking powder and salt. Add dry ingredients to creamed mixture; stir until a soft dough forms. Shape dough into 1-inch balls and place 2 inches apart on a greased baking sheet; flatten balls into 2-inch-diameter cookies with the bottom of a glass dipped in sugar. Bake 7 to 9 minutes or until bottoms are lightly browned. Transfer cookies to a wire rack to cool.

For icing, combine shortening, confectioners sugar, vanilla and milk in a large bowl; beat until smooth. Spoon icing into pastry bag fitted with a small star tip. Pipe snowflake design onto each cookie. Let icing harden. Store in an airtight container

YIELD: About 9 dozen cookies

8

Cinnamon Nut Cookies

1 cup butter or margarine, softened
1 cup extra-crunchy peanut butter
3/4 cup firmly packed brown sugar
3/4 cup granulated sugar
2 eggs
1-1/2 teaspoons vanilla extract
2-1/2 cups all-purpose flour
1 teaspoon baking powder
1 teaspoon baking soda
1/2 teaspoon salt
1-1/2 cups coarsely crushed cinnamon graham crackers (about 22 squares), divided
1/2 cup finely chopped dry-roasted peanuts

Preheat oven to 350 degrees. In a large bowl, cream butter, peanut butter and sugars until fluffy. Add eggs and vanilla; beat until smooth. In a medium bowl, combine flour, baking powder, baking soda and salt. Add dry ingredients to creamed mixture; beat until well blended. Stir in 1 cup cracker crumbs.

In a small bowl, combine remaining 1/2 cup cracker crumbs and peanuts. Roll heaping teaspoonfuls of dough into balls; roll in crumb mixture. Place balls on a lightly greased baking sheet; flatten with a fork. Bake 7 to 9 minutes or until lightly browned. Transfer to a wire rack to cool. Store in an airtight container.

YIELD: about 7 dozen cookies

9

Easy Coconut Macaroons

2 cups all-purpose baking mix
1 can (14 oz) sweetened condensed milk
1 egg
1 teaspoon vanilla extract
1 can (3-1/2 oz) flaked coconut
Vegetable cooking spray
2 tablespoons sugar
5 oz red candied cherries, halved

Preheat oven to 350 degrees. In a large bowl, combine baking mix, sweetened condensed milk, egg and vanilla; beat until well blended. Stir in coconut. Drop teaspoonfuls of dough onto a cookie sheet sprayed with cooking spray. Sprinkle tops of cookies with sugar. Bake 6 to 8 minutes or until bottoms are golden brown. Press a cherry half into center of each warm cookie. Transfer cookies to a wire rack to cool. Store in an airtight container.

YIELD: about 6 dozen cookies

10

Cranberry Christmas Cookies

1 cup fresh cranberries
1/2 cup vegetable shortening
1-1/2 cups sugar
1 egg
2 tablespoons buttermilk
1 teaspoons vanilla extract
1/4 teaspoon orange extract
2 cups all-purpose flour
1/2 teaspoon baking soda
1/2 teaspoon ground cinnamon
1/2 teaspoon ground cloves
1/2 teaspoon ground nutmeg
1/4 teaspoon salt
1 cup chopped walnuts
1 cup golden raisins

Preheat oven to 375 degrees. Process cranberries in a food processor until coarsely ground. In a large bowl, cream shortening and sugar until fluffy. Add egg, buttermilk and extracts; beat until smooth. Stir in cranberries.

In a small bowl, combine flour, baking soda, cinnamon, cloves, nutmeg, and salt. Add dry ingredients to creamed mixture; stir until a soft dough forms. Stir in walnuts and raisins. Drop teaspoonfuls of dough onto a greased baking sheet. Bake 9 to 11 minutes or until bottoms are lightly browned. Transfer cookies to a wire rack to cool. Store in an airtight container.

YIELD: about 7 dozen cookies

11

Gingerbread Cookie Rounds

COOKIES

- 1/2 cup butter or margarine, softened
- 1/2 cup firmly packed brown sugar
- 1/2 cup granulated sugar
- 1/2 cup molasses
- 1/4 cup strongly brewed coffee
- 1 egg
- 1 teaspoon vanilla extract
- 3 cups all-purpose flour
- 1/4 cup cocoa
- 1-1/2 teaspoons ground ginger
- 1 teaspoon ground cinnamon
- 1 teaspoon baking soda
- 1/4 teaspoon ground cloves
- 1/4 teaspoon salt

ICING

- 1/2 cup sifted confectioners sugar
- 1 tablespoon vegetable shortening
- 1 tablespoon butter or margarine, softened
- 1–2 teaspoons water
- 1/4 teaspoon vanilla extract

For cookies, cream butter and sugars in a large bowl until fluffy. Add molasses, coffee, egg and vanilla; beat until smooth. In a medium bowl combine flour, cocoa, ginger, cinnamon, baking soda, cloves and salt. Add dry ingredients to creamed mixture; stir until a soft dough forms. Cover and chill one hour.

Preheat oven to 350 degrees. On a lightly floured surface, use a floured rolling pan to roll out dough to 1/8-inch thickness. Use a floured 3-inch-diameter fluted-edge cookie cutter to cut out cookies. Transfer to a greased baking sheet. Bake 6 to 8 minutes or until bottoms are lightly browned. Transfer to a wire rack to cool completely.

For icing, beat confectioners sugar, shortening, butter, water and vanilla in a small bowl until smooth. Spoon icing into a pastry bag fitted with a small round tip. Pipe desired decorations onto cookies. Let icing harden. Store in an airtight container.

YIELD: about 3-1/2 dozen cookies

12

Holiday Spritz Cookies

1 cup butter, softened
1 cup sugar
3 oz cream cheese, softened
1 egg
1 teaspoon vanilla extract
2-1/3 cups all-purpose flour
1/2 teaspoon baking powder
1/4 teaspoon salt
2 tablespoons green non-pareils
2 tablespoons red non-pareils

Preheat oven to 375 degrees. In a large bowl, combine butter, sugar, cream cheese, egg and vanilla; beat until smooth. Sift flour, baking powder and salt into a medium bowl. Add dry ingredients to creamed mixture; beat until well blended. Stir in non-pareils. Spoon dough into a cookie press fitted with a tree disc. Press cookies onto an ungreased baking sheet. Bake for 5 to 7 minutes or until bottoms are very lightly browned. Transfer cookies to a wire rack to cool. Store in an airtight container

YIELD: about 8 dozen cookies

13

Lemon Lace Cookies

2 cups butter or margarine, softened
1-1/4 cups sugar
1 tablespoon grated lemon zest
1 teaspoon lemon extract
1 teaspoon vanilla extract
3 cups quick-cooking oats
2 cups all-purpose flour
1/2 teaspoon salt
Confectioners sugar

In a large bowl, cream butter and sugar until fluffy. Beat in lemon zest and extracts. In a medium bowl, combine oats, flour and salt. Add dry ingredients to creamed mixture; stir until a soft dough forms. Cover and chill 30 minutes.

Preheat oven to 350 degrees. Shape dough into 1-inch balls; place about 2 inches apart on an ungreased baking sheet. Flatten balls with bottom of a glass dipped in confectioners sugar. Bake 9 to 11 minutes or until edges are lightly browned. Cool cookies on baking sheet 1 minute; transfer to wire rack to cool completely. Store in an airtight container.

YIELD: About 8 dozen cookies

14

Orange-Nut Bars

CRUST

1-1/2 cups all-purpose flour

1/2 cups sifted confectioners sugar

2/3 cup chopped pecans, toasted and coarsely ground

3/4 cup butter or margarine, chilled

FILLING

1-3/4 cups sugar

4 eggs

1/3 cup orange juice

1/2 teaspoon orange extract

1/4 cup all-purpose flour

1/4 teaspoon baking powder

Preheat oven to 350 degrees. For crust, combine flour, confectioners sugar and pecans in a medium bowl. Using a pastry blender or 2 knives, cut in butter until well blended. With lightly greased hands, press crust into bottom and 1/4 inch up sides of a greased 9 x 13-inch baking pan. Bake 20 minutes.

For filling, combine sugar, eggs, orange juice and orange extract in a medium bowl; whisk until well blended. In a small bowl, combine flour and baking powder. Add dry ingredients to sugar mixture; whisk until well blended. Pour mixture over warm crust. Return to oven and bake 25 to 30 minutes longer or until filling is set. Cool in pan on a wire rack. Cut into 1 x 2-inch bars. Store in a single layer in an airtight container in the refrigerator.

YIELD: about 4 dozen bars

15

Peanut Butter Chocolate Chip Cookies

1/2 cup butter or margarine, softened
1/2 cup crunchy peanut butter
1/2 cup firmly packed brown sugar
1/2 cup granulated sugar
1 egg
1 teaspoon vanilla extract
1-2/3 cups all-purpose flour
1/2 teaspoon baking powder
1/4 teaspoon salt
1 cup semi-sweet chocolate mini chips

Preheat oven to 375 degrees. In a large bowl, cream butter, peanut butter and sugars until fluffy. Add egg and vanilla; beat until smooth. In a small bowl, combine flour, baking powder and salt. Add dry ingredients to creamed mixture; stir until a soft dough forms. Stir in chocolate chips. Divide dough into thirds. Shape each third into a 7-inch long roll. With a serrated knife, cut dough into 1/4-inch slices. Place on an ungreased baking sheet. Bake 7 to 9 minutes or until bottoms are golden brown. Transfer to a wire rack to cool. Store in an airtight container.

YIELD: about 2 dozen cookies per roll

16

Peppermint Swirl Cookies

1 package (16.5 oz) refrigerated sugar cookie dough
1/4 cup finely crushed peppermint candies (about 10 round candies)
1/8 teaspoon red liquid food coloring

Divide sugar cookie dough in half. On a sheet of plastic wrap, use a floured rolling pin to roll out half the dough into an 8-inch square. Knead peppermint candies and food coloring into remaining half of dough.

On a separate sheet of plastic wrap, roll out peppermint dough into an 8-inch square. Place peppermint dough on top of plain dough. Using plastic wrap, roll dough into an 8-inch long roll. Chill 2 hours.

Preheat oven to 350 degrees. With a serrated knife, cut dough into 1/4-inch slices. Place 2 inches apart on a lightly greased baking sheet. Bake 8 to 10 minutes. Cool cookies on baking sheet 5 minutes; transfer to a wire rack to cool completely. Store in an airtight container.

YIELD: about 2-1/2 dozen cookies

17

Pudding Cookies

1 cup butter or margarine, softened
1/2 cup granulated sugar
1/2 cup firmly packed brown sugar
2 eggs
2 teaspoons vanilla extract
2-1/2 cups all-purpose flour
1 teaspoon baking soda
1/4 teaspoon salt
Instant pudding mix *(see below)*
Flavored baking chips *(see below)*

Preheat oven to 350 degrees. In a large bowl, cream butter and sugars until fluffy. Add eggs and vanilla; beat until smooth. In a medium bowl, combine flour, baking soda, salt, pudding mix and flavored baking chips. Add dry ingredients to creamed mixture; stir until a soft dough forms. Drop by tablespoonfuls onto a lightly greased baking sheet. Bake 9 to 11 minutes or until bottoms are lightly browned. Transfer cookies to a wire rack to cool. Store in an airtight container.

YIELD: about 4 dozen cookies

Chocolate: 3.9 oz package chocolate instant putting mix and 6 oz package semi-sweet chocolate chips

Butterscotch: 3.5 oz package butterscotch instant pudding mix and 8 oz package almond brickle chips

18

Quick Gingerbread Cookies

1 package (16.5 oz) refrigerated sugar cookie dough
2 teaspoons molasses
1/4 to 1/2 cup all-purpose flour, divided
1 tablespoon ground cinnamon
1/8 teaspoon ground ginger
1–2 teaspoons cocoa
Desired shape cookie cutter, about 3-1/2 x 4-inches

Preheat oven to 350 degrees. Flatten dough on a lightly floured surface. Drizzle molasses over dough. Sprinkle 1/4 cup flour, cinnamon, ginger and cocoa over the dough. Knead ingredients into dough until well blended, using additional flour as necessary. On a lightly floured surface, use a floured rolling pin to roll out dough to 1/4-inch thickness. Use cookie cutter to cut out dough. Transfer to a greased baking sheet. Bake 6 to 8 minutes or until bottoms are lightly browned. Transfer to a wire rack to cool. Store in an airtight container

YIELD: about 1 dozen cookies

19

Round Ornament Cookies

COOKIES
- 1/2 cup butter or margarine, softened
- 1/3 cup vegetable shortening
- 1/2 cup granulated sugar
- 1/2 cup firmly packed brown sugar
- 1/4 cup dark corn syrup
- 1 egg
- 1 teaspoon vanilla extract
- 3 cups all-purpose flour
- 1/4 teaspoon salt

ICING
- 6-2/3 cups confectioners sugar
- 1/2 cup water
- 1 tablespoon light corn syrup
- 1 teaspoon vanilla extract
- Red, green, yellow and blue paste food coloring

For cookies, cream butter, shortening and sugars in a large bowl until fluffy. Add corn syrup, egg and vanilla; beat until smooth. In a medium bowl, combine flour and salt. Add dry ingredients to creamed mixture; stir until a soft dough forms. Divide dough in half. On a lightly floured surface, use a floured rolling pin to roll out half of dough to 1/8-inch thickness. To cut each cookie, use a sharp knife to draw around a glass that is about 2-1/2-inch diameter, cutting a small ornament cap on the circle to make the cookie have an ornament shape. Transfer to a greased baking sheet. Use a drinking straw or skewer to make a hole in top of each cookie. Bake 6 to 8 minutes or until bottoms are lightly browned. Transfer cookies to a wire rack to cool. Repeat with remaining dough.

For icing, combine confectioners sugar, water, corn syrup and vanilla in a medium bowl; stir until smooth. Place 1/4 cup white icing in a small bowl and cover. Divide remaining icing into four small bowls; tint icing red, green, yellow and blue. Spoon icing into pastry bags fitted with small round tips. Use tinted icing to pipe outline around edges of cookies; fill in with icing. Let icing harden. Use white icing to pipe a highlight onto each cookie. Let icing harden. Store in a single layer in an airtight container.

YIELD: about 4-1/4 dozen cookies

20

Slice & Bake Cookies

3/4 cup butter or margarine, softened
1-1/4 cups sugar
1 egg
1 teaspoon vanilla extract
2 cups all-purpose flour
1/2 teaspoon salt

In a large bowl, cream butter and sugar until fluffy. Add egg and vanilla; beat until smooth. In a small bowl, combine flour and salt. Add dry ingredients to creamed mixture; stir until a soft dough forms. Divide dough in half. Place each half on plastic wrap. Use plastic wrap to shape dough into two 8-inch long rolls. Chill three hours or until firm (if rolls have flattened, reshape into a round shape).

Preheat oven to 375 degrees. Using a serrated knife, cut dough into 1/4-inch slices. Place 1 inch apart on a lightly greased baking sheet. Bake 6 to 8 minutes or until bottoms are lightly browned. Transfer cookies to a wire rack to cool. Store in an airtight container.

YIELD: about 5 dozen cookies

21

Snowman Cookies

COOKIES

- 3/4 cup butter or margarine, softened
- 3 oz cream cheese, softened
- 1 cup granulated sugar
- 1/2 cup confectioners sugar
- 1 egg
- 1 teaspoon almond extract
- 2-3/4 cups all-purpose flour
- 1/2 teaspoon baking powder
- 1/4 teaspoon salt

ICING

- 2-1/2 cups confectioners sugar
- 3-1/2–4 tablespoons milk
- 1/2 teaspoon almond extract
- Green, black, orange and red paste food coloring

Preheat oven to 375 degrees. For cookies, cream butter, cream cheese and sugars in a large bowl until fluffy. Add egg and almond extract; beat until smooth. In a medium bowl, combine flour, baking powder and salt. Add dry ingredients to creamed mixture; stir until a soft dough forms. On a lightly floured surface, use a floured rolling pin to roll out dough to 3/8-inch thickness. Use a 4-1/4 x 5-1/4-inch gingerbread boy cookie cutter to cut out cookies. Place 2 inches apart on a lightly greased baking sheet. Bake 8 to 10 minutes or until bottoms are lightly browned. Cool cookies on baking sheet 2 minutes; transfer to a wire rack to cool completely.

For icing, combine confectioners sugar, milk and almond extract in a small bowl; stir until smooth. Transfer 3 tablespoons icing into each of 3 small bowls; tint green, black and orange. Tint remaining icing red. Spoon icing into pastry bags fitted with small round tips. Use black icing to pipe eyes and mouth onto cookies. Use orange icing to pipe "carrot" noses. Use red icing to pipe scarves and boots. Use green icing to pipe mittens and buttons. Let icing harden. Store in a single layer between sheets of wax paper in an airtight container.

YIELD: about 1 dozen cookies

22

Spicy Christmas Hearts

3/4 cup butter or margarine, softened
1/3 cup firmly packed brown sugar
1/3 cup granulated sugar
1 cup molasses
3-1/2 cups all-purpose flour
3/4 teaspoon baking soda
3/4 teaspoon ground cinnamon
3/4 teaspoon ground cloves
1/4 teaspoon salt
Granulated sugar to decorate

In a large bowl, cream butter, brown sugar and 1/3 cup granulated sugar until fluffy. Add molasses; beat until smooth. In a medium bowl, combine flour, baking soda, cinnamon, cloves and salt. Gradually add dry ingredients to creamed mixture; stir until a soft dough forms. Divide dough into fourths. Wrap in plastic wrap and chill 8 hours or overnight.

Preheat oven to 350 degrees. On a lightly floured surface, use a floured rolling pin to roll out one fourth of the dough to 1/8-inch thickness. Use a 2-1/4-inch-wide heart-shaped cookie cutter to cut out cookies. Transfer to a greased baking sheet. Sprinkle cookies with granulated sugar. Bake 6 to 8 minutes or until edges are lightly browned. Transfer cookies to a wire rack to cool. Repeat with remaining dough. Store in an airtight container.

YIELD: about 10 dozen cookies

23

Star Cookies

3/4 cup butter or margarine, softened
1/2 cup sugar
1 egg
1 teaspoon vanilla extract
1-3/4 cups all-purpose flour
3 tablespoons cornstarch
1/2 teaspoon baking powder
1/8 teaspoon salt

Preheat oven to 350 degrees. In a medium bowl, cream butter and sugar until fluffy. Add egg and vanilla; beat until smooth. In a small bowl, combine flour, cornstarch, baking powder and salt. Add dry ingredients to creamed mixture; stir until a soft dough forms. On a lightly floured surface, use a floured rolling pin to roll out dough to 1/8-inch thickness. Use a 2-3/4-inch-wide star-shaped cookie cutter to cut out cookies. Transfer to a greased baking sheet. Bake 7 to 9 minutes or until bottoms are lightly browned. Transfer cookies to a wire rack to cool. Store in an airtight container.

YIELD: about 4 dozen cookies.

Sugarplum Cookies

4 cups sifted confectioners sugar
3-1/2 to 4 tablespoons water
1 tablespoon light corn syrup
1 teaspoon vanilla extract
Green and red paste food coloring
1 package (11 ounces) sugar cookies (about 2 inches in diameter)

In a medium bowl, combine confectioners sugar, water, corn syrup and vanilla; beat until smooth. Transfer about 1/2 cup icing into each of 3 small bowls. Tint green and red, leaving remaining icing white. Spoon each icing into a pastry bag fitted with a small round tip. Working with 3 cookies at a time, outline and fill in and tops of cookies with a thin layer of green or red icing. While icing is still wet, pipe white icing onto cookies in a spiral design. Place on a wire rack to let icing harden. Store in an airtight container.

YIELD: about 2 dozen cookies

HOLIDAY TRIVIA!

According to Clarence in the classic movie, It's a Wonderful Life, what happens every time a bell rings?

— ANSWER FOUND ON PAGE 127 —

25

Toffee Almond Cookies

1 cup butter or margarine, softened
2 cups firmly packed brown sugar
2 eggs
1 teaspoon almond extract
1 teaspoon vanilla extract
3 cups all-purpose flour
1 teaspoon baking powder
1/2 teaspoon salt
1 package (8 oz) almond brickle chips
1 cup slivered almonds, toasted

Preheat oven to 350 degrees. In a large bowl, cream butter and brown sugar until fluffy. Add eggs and extracts; beat until smooth. In a medium bowl, combine flour, baking powder and salt. Add dry ingredients to creamed mixture; beat until well blended. Stir in brickle chips and almonds. Drop by heaping teaspoonfuls onto a greased baking sheet. Bake 8 to 10 minutes or until bottoms are lightly browned. Transfer cookies to a wire rack to cool. Store in an airtight container.

YIELD: About 7 dozen cookies

Holiday Beverages

Nothing takes the chill out of the crisp holiday air like a cozy sweater and a warm beverage. Whether you are caroling around a fire in the backyard, ice skating on the local pond or sledding down the largest hill in the neighborhood—pack a thermos with the hot drinks included in this section to warm the fingers, toes and hearts of your friends and family. No mittens required!

Almond Cocoa

1 cup butter
1 cup granulated sugar
1 cup firmly packed brown sugar
2/3 cup cocoa
2 cups softened vanilla ice cream
2-1/2 teaspoons almond extract
12 cups boiling water or hot coffee

In a medium saucepan, combine butter, sugars and cocoa over low heat. Stirring frequently, cook until butter melts. Transfer mixture to a medium bowl. Add ice cream and almond extract; beat until smooth. Store in an airtight container in refrigerator until ready to serve. To serve, pour cocoa mixture into a large serving bowl. Pour boiling water or hot coffee into the mixture and stir until well blended.

YIELD: About 16 servings

HOLIDAY TRIVIA!

How many ghosts visit Scrooge in A Christmas Carol and what are their names?

— ANSWER FOUND ON PAGE 127 —

Holiday Coffee

1/3 cup ground coffee
2 cinnamon sticks, broken into pieces
6 whole cloves
1 vanilla bean (about 3 inches long)
1-1/2 quarts water

Combine coffee, cinnamon pieces and cloves in an airtight container. Split vanilla bean and scrape seeds into mixture. Cut vanilla bean into 3 pieces and add to mixture. Cover and store in refrigerator overnight to allow flavors to blend.

To serve, brew coffee mixture and water in a 10-cup coffee maker. Serve hot.

YIELD: about eight 6-ounce servings

HOLIDAY TRIVIA!

In which Christmas carol do the names Little Nell and Little Will appear?

— ANSWER FOUND ON PAGE 127 —

Cinnamon Mocha

1 jar (16 oz) non-dairy powdered creamer
2-1/3 cups chocolate milk mix
1 package (16 oz) confectioners sugar
6 cups instant nonfat dry milk
1/2 cup cocoa
1/4 cup instant coffee granules
2 teaspoons ground cinnamon

In a very large bowl, combine creamer, chocolate mix, confectioners sugar, dry milk, cocoa, coffee granules and cinnamon. Store in an airtight container. To serve, pour 3/4 cup hot water over 2-1/2 heaping tablespoons mocha mix; stir until well blended.

YIELD: about 14 cups mix (about 75 servings)

Hazelnut Mocha

1 package (25.6 oz) instant nonfat dry milk
1 package (16 oz) confectioners sugar, sifted
2-1/3 cups chocolate milk mix
1 jar (11 oz) non-dairy powdered creamer
1 jar (15 oz) hazelnut-flavored non-dairy powdered creamer
1/2 cup cocoa
1/4 cup instant coffee granules

In a very large bowl, combine dry milk, confectioners sugar, chocolate milk mix, creamers, cocoa and coffee granules; stir until well blended. Store in an airtight container. To serve, pour 3/4 cup hot water over 3 tablespoons mocha mix; stir until well blended.

YIELD: about 18-1/4 cups mocha mix (about 95 servings)

Silver Bells Punch

1 can (46 oz) unsweetened pineapple juice, chilled
2 cups piña colada drink mixer, chilled
1 can (12 oz) frozen orange juice concentrate, thawed
1 liter club soda, chilled
1 liter lemon-lime soda, chilled
1 package (10 oz) frozen raspberries in syrup, slightly thawed

In a punch bowl, stir together pineapple juice, piña colada mixer, orange juice, club soda and lemon-lime soda. Stir in raspberries. Serve chilled.

YIELD: about 24 6-oz servings

HOLIDAY TRIVIA!

Which U.S. state was the first to recognize Christmas as a holiday?

— ANSWER FOUND ON PAGE 127 —

Holiday Songs

Christmas Carol Lyrics

Perhaps one of the most cherished holiday traditions is that of joining together in song to celebrate the season of peace and goodwill. There is just something so heartwarming and joyous about singing the carols that we grew up with, sang in church and taught our children.

On the following pages, you'll find lyrics to twenty-five classic holiday songs. From *Deck the Halls* and *Silent Night* to *Jingle Bells*—there's something for all ages. Of course, there are many songs that people may know the chorus to, but having the lyrics to all of the verses comes in quite handy. You might even find that guests sing a little louder when they have the confidence of a book in their hand (and something to hide behind if they are shy!). Moreover, your group is sure to be the most festive with matching songbooks.

The songs are numbered for your convenience. You can plan the order ahead of time or appoint a leader to call out the song number as you go. If you are travelling in the neighborhood, be sure all carolers have arrived at the door before ringing the doorbell.

LET THE
MERRY-MAKING
BEGIN!

ANGELS WE HAVE HEARD ON HIGH

1

Angels we have heard on high
Sweetly singing o'er the plains
And the mountains in reply
Echoing their joyous strains
Gloria, in excelsis Deo!
Gloria, in excelsis Deo!

Shepherds, why this jubilee?
Why your joyous strains prolong?
What the gladsome tidings be?
Which inspire your heavenly songs?
Gloria, in excelsis Deo!
Gloria, in excelsis Deo!

Come to Bethlehem and see
Him whose birth the angels sing;
Come, adore on bended knee,
Christ the Lord, the newborn King.
Gloria, in excelsis Deo!
Gloria, in excelsis Deo!

See Him in a manger laid,
Jesus, Lord of heaven and earth;
Mary, Joseph, lend your aid,
With us sing our Savior's birth.
Gloria, in excelsis Deo!
Gloria, in excelsis Deo!

AULD Lang Syne

2

Should old acquaintance be forgot,
and never brought to mind?
Should old acquaintance be forgot,
and old lang syne?

CHORUS:
For auld lang syne, my dear,
for auld lang syne,
we'll take a cup of kindness yet,
for auld lang syne.

And surely you'll buy your pint cup!
and surely I'll buy mine!
And we'll take a cup o' kindness yet,
for auld lang syne.
(repeat chorus)

We two have run about the slopes,
and picked the daisies fine;
But we've wandered many a weary foot,
since auld lang syne.
(repeat chorus)

We two have paddled in the stream,
from morning sun till dine;
But seas between us broad have roared
since auld lang syne.
(repeat chorus)

And there's a hand my trusty friend!
And give me a hand o' thine!
And we'll take a right good-will draught,
for auld lang syne.
(repeat chorus)

Away In A Manger

3

Away in a manger, no crib for a bed,
The little Lord Jesus lay down his sweet head.
The stars in the bright sky looked down where he lay,
The little Lord Jesus asleep on the hay.

The cattle are lowing, the baby awakes,
But little Lord Jesus, no crying he makes.
I love thee, Lord Jesus! look down from the sky,
And stay by my cradle till morning is nigh.

Be near me, Lord Jesus; I ask thee to stay
Close by me forever, and love me I pray.
Bless all the dear children in thy tender care,
And take us to heaven to live with thee there.

DECK
THE
HALLS

4

Deck the halls with boughs of holly,
Fa, la, la, la, la, la, la, la, la!
'Tis the season to be jolly,
Fa, la, la, la, la, la, la, la, la!
Don we now our gay apparel,
Fa, la, la, la, la, la, la, la!
Troll the ancient Yule-tide carol,
Fa, la, la, la, la, la, la, la!

See the blazing yule before us,
Fa, la, la, la, la, la, la, la, la!
Strike the harp and join the chorus.
Fa, la, la, la, la, la, la, la, la!
Follow me in merry measure,
Fa, la, la, la, la, la, la, la!
While I tell of Yule-tide treasure,
Fa, la, la, la, la, la, la, la, la!

Fast away the old year passes,
Fa, la, la, la, la, la, la, la, la!
Hail the new, ye lads and lasses!
Fa, la, la, la, la, la, la, la, la!
Sing we joyous all together,
Fa, la, la, la, la, la, la, la!
Heedless of the wind and weather,
Fa, la, la, la, la, la, la, la, la!

DING DONG
Merrily
ON HIGH

5

Ding dong merrily on high,
In heav'n the bells are ringing:
Ding dong! verily the sky
Is riv'n with angel singing
Gloria Hosanna in excelsis!
Gloria Hosanna in excelsis!

E'en so here below, below,
Let steeple bells be swungen,
And "Io, io, io!"
By priest and people sungen
Gloria Hosanna in excelsis!
Gloria Hosanna in excelsis!

Pray you, dutifully prime
Your matin chime, ye ringers,
May you beautifully rhyme
Your eve'time song, ye singers
Gloria Hosanna in excelsis!
Gloria Hosanna in excelsis!

Gloria Hosanna in excelsis!
Gloria Hosanna in excelsis!
Hosanna in excelsis!!!

Good King Wenceslas

6

Good King Wenceslas looked out, on the Feast of Stephen,
When the snow lay round about, deep and crisp and even;
Brightly shone the moon that night, tho' the frost was cruel,
When a poor man came in sight, gath'ring winter fuel.

"Hither, page, and stand by me, if thou know'st it, telling,
Yonder peasant, who is he? Where and what his dwelling?"
"Sire, he lives a good league hence, underneath the mountain;
Right against the forest fence, by Saint Agnes' fountain."

"Bring me flesh, and bring me wine, bring me pine logs hither:
Thou and I shall see him dine, when we bear them thither."
Page and monarch, forth they went, forth they went together;
Through the rude wind's wild lament and the bitter weather.

"Sire, the night is darker now, and the wind blows stronger;
Fails my heart, I know not how; I can go no longer."
"Mark my footsteps, good my page. Tread thou in them boldly
Thou shalt find the winter's rage freeze thy blood less coldly."

In his master's steps he trod, where the snow lay dinted;
Heat was in the very sod which the saint had printed.
Therefore, Christian men, be sure, wealth or rank possessing,
Ye who now will bless the poor, shall yourselves find blessing.

HARK! THE HERALD ANGELS SING

7

Hark! The herald angels sing
"Glory to the newborn king;
Peace on earth and mercy mild,
God and sinners reconciled"
Joyful all ye nations rise,
Join the triumph of the skies
With the angelic host proclaim
"Christ is born in Bethlehem"
Hark! The herald-angels sing
"Glory to the newborn king"

Christ, by highest heaven adored
Christ, the everlasting Lord,
Late in time behold Him come
Offspring of a Virgin's womb:
Veiled in flesh the Godhead see,
Hail the incarnate Deity
Pleased as man with man to dwell
Jesus, our Emmanuel
Hark! The herald-angels sing
"Glory to the newborn king"

Hail the Heaven-born Prince of Peace!
Hail the Son of Righteousness!
Light and life to all He brings,
Risen with healing in His wings;
Mild He lays His glory by
Born that man no more may die
Born to raise the sons of earth
Born to give them second birth
Hark! The herald-angels sing
"Glory to the newborn king"

HERE
WE COME
A-Caroling

8

Here we come a-caroling
Among the leaves so green,
Here we come a wand'ring,
So fair to be seen.

CHORUS:
Love and joy come to you,
And to you glad Christmas too
And God bless you and send you a Happy New Year,
And God send you a Happy New Year.

We are not daily beggars
Who beg from door to door,
But we are friendly neighbors
Whom you have seen before.
(repeat chorus)

God bless the Master of this house,
Likewise the Mistress too
And all the little children,
That round the table go.
(repeat chorus)

I Heard The Bells On Christmas Day

9

I heard the bells on Christmas Day
Their old, familiar carols play,
and wild and sweet
The words repeat
Of peace on earth, good will to men!

I thought how as the day had come
The belfries of all Christendom
Had roll'd along
th' unbroken song
Of peace on earth, good will to men!

And in despair I bowed my head;
"There is no peace on earth," I said;
"For hate is strong,
And mocks the song
Of peace on earth, good will to men!"

Then pealed the bells more loud and deep:
"God is not dead, nor doth He sleep;
The wrong shall fail,
The right prevail,
With peace on earth, good will to men."

IT CAME UPON A MIDNIGHT CLEAR

10

It came upon a midnight clear,
That glorious song of old,
From angels bending near the earth,
To touch their harps of gold:
"Peace on the earth, goodwill to men,
From heaven's all-gracious King."
The world in solemn stillness lay,
To hear the angels sing.

Still through the cloven skies they come,
With peaceful wings unfurled,
And still their heavenly music floats
O'er all the weary world;
Above its sad and lowly plains,
They bend on hovering wing,
And ever o'er its babel sounds
The blessed angels sing.

Yet with the woes of sin and strife
The world has suffered long;
Beneath the angel-strain have rolled
Two thousand years of wrong;
And man, at war with man, hears not
The love-song which they bring;
O hush the noise, ye men of strife,
And hear the angels sing.

And ye, beneath life's crushing load,
Whose forms are bending low,
Who toil along the climbing way
With painful steps and slow,
Look now! for glad and golden hours
come swiftly on the wing.
O rest beside the weary road,
And hear the angels sing!

For lo!, the days are hastening on,
By prophet bards foretold,
When with the ever-circling years
Comes round the age of gold
When peace shall over all the earth
Its ancient splendors fling,
And the whole world give back the song
Which now the angels sing.

JINGLE Bells

11

Dashing through the snow
In a one-horse open sleigh
O'er the fields we go
Laughing all the way

Bells on bob tail ring
Making spirits bright
What fun it is to ride and sing
A sleighing song tonight!

CHORUS:
Jingle bells, jingle bells,
Jingle all the way.
Oh! what fun it is to ride
In a one-horse open sleigh.
Jingle bells, jingle bells,
Jingle all the way;
Oh! what fun it is to ride
In a one-horse open sleigh.

A day or two ago
I thought I'd take a ride
And soon, Miss Fanny Bright
Was seated by my side,
The horse was lean and lank
Misfortune seemed his lot
He got into a drifted bank
And then we got upsot.
(repeat chorus)

A day or two ago,
The story I must tell
I went out on the snow,
And on my back I fell;
A gent was riding by
In a one-horse open sleigh,
He laughed as there I sprawling lie,
But quickly drove away.
(repeat chorus)

Now the ground is white
Go it while you're young,
Take the girls tonight
and sing this sleighing song;
Just get a bobtailed bay
Two forty as his speed
Hitch him to an open sleigh
And crack! you'll take the lead.
(repeat chorus)

Jolly Old Saint Nicholas

12

Jolly old Saint Nicholas
Lean your ear this way;
Don't you tell a single soul
What I'm going to say,
Christmas Eve is coming soon;
Now you dear old man,
Whisper what you'll bring to me;
Tell me if you can.

When the clock is striking twelve,
When I'm fast asleep,
Down the chimney broad and black
With your pack you'll creep;
All the stockings you will find
Hanging in a row;
Mine will be the shortest one;
You'll be sure to know.

Johnny wants a pair of skates;
Suzy wants a sled.
Nellie wants a picture book,
Yellow, blue and red.
Now I think I'll leave to you
What to give the rest.
Choose for me, dear Santa Claus,
You will know best.

JOY TO THE WORLD

13

Joy to the World; the Lord is come!
Let earth receive her King!
Let ev'ry heart prepare Him room,
And Heaven and nature sing.
And Heaven and nature sing.
And Heaven and nature sing.

Joy to the earth, the Savior reigns!
Let men their songs employ;
While fields & floods, rocks, hills & plains
Repeat the sounding joy.
Repeat the sounding joy.
Repeat the sounding joy.

No more let sins and sorrows grow,
Nor thorns infest the ground;
He comes to make his blessings flow
Far as the curse is found.
Far as the curse is found.
Far as the curse is found.

He rules the world with truth and grace,
And makes the nations prove
The glories of His righteousness,
And wonders of His love.
And wonders of His love.
And wonders of His love.

O Christmas
TREE

14

O Christmas tree, O Christmas tree!
How lovely are thy branches!
O Christmas tree, O Christmas tree,
How lovely are thy branches!

Not only green when summer's here,
But in the coldest time of year.
O Christmas tree, O Christmas tree,
How lovely are thy branches!

O Christmas tree, O Christmas tree,
Much pleasure doth thou bring me!
O Christmas tree, O Christmas tree,
Much pleasure doth thou bring me!

For every year the Christmas tree,
Brings to us all both joy and glee.
O Christmas tree, O Christmas tree,
Much pleasure doth thou bring me!

O Christmas tree, O Christmas tree,
How sturdy God hath made thee!
O Christmas tree, O Christmas tree,
How sturdy God hath made thee!

Thou bidd'st us all place faithfully
Our trust in God, unchangingly!
O Christmas tree, O Christmas tree,
How sturdy God hath made thee!

O Christmas tree, O Christmas tree,
Thy candles shine out brightly!
O Christmas tree, O Christmas tree,
Thy candles shine out brightly!

Each bough doth hold its tiny light,
That makes each toy to sparkle bright.
O Christmas tree, O Christmas tree,
Thy candles shine out brightly!

O Come, All Ye Faithful

15

O come, all ye faithful, joyful and triumphant!
O come ye, O come ye to Bethlehem;
Come and behold him
Born the King of Angels:
O come, let us adore Him,
O come, let us adore Him,
O come, let us adore Him,
Christ the Lord.

God of God, light of light,
Lo, he abhors not the Virgin's womb;
True God, begotten, not created:
O come, let us adore Him,
O come, let us adore Him,
O come, let us adore Him,
Christ the Lord.

Sing, choirs of angels, sing in exultation,
Sing, all ye citizens of Heaven above!
Glory to God, glory in the highest:
O come, let us adore Him,
O come, let us adore Him,
O come, let us adore Him,
Christ the Lord.

Yea, Lord, we greet thee, born this happy morning;
Jesus, to thee be glory given!
Word of the Father, now in flesh appearing!
O come, let us adore Him,
O come, let us adore Him,
O come, let us adore Him,
Christ the Lord.

O COME, O COME, EMMANUEL

16

O come, O come, Emmanuel,
And ransom captive Israel,
That mourns in lonely exile here,
Until the Son of God appear.
Rejoice! Rejoice! Emmanuel
Shall come to thee, O Israel.

O come, Thou Rod of Jesse, free
Thine own from Satan's tyranny;
From depths of hell Thy people save,
And give them victory o'er the grave.
Rejoice! Rejoice! Emmanuel
Shall come to thee, O Israel.

O come, Thou Dayspring, from on high,
And cheer us by Thy drawing nigh;
Disperse the gloomy clouds of night,
And death's dark shadows put to flight.
Rejoice! Rejoice! Emmanuel
Shall come to thee, O Israel.

O come, Thou Key of David, come
And open wide our heav'nly home;
Make safe the way that leads on high,
And close the path to misery.
Rejoice! Rejoice! Emmanuel
Shall come to thee, O Israel.

O come, Adonai, Lord of might,
Who to Thy tribes, on Sinai's height,
In ancient times didst give the law
In cloud and majesty and awe.
Rejoice! Rejoice! Emmanuel
Shall come to thee, O Israel.

O Holy Night

17

O holy night! The stars are brightly shining,
It is the night of our dear Savior's birth.
Long lay the world in sin and error pining,
Till He appear'd and the soul felt its worth.
A thrill of hope, the weary world rejoices,
For yonder breaks a new and glorious morn.

Fall on your knees! O hear the angel voices!
O night divine, O night when Christ was born;
O night divine, O night, O night Divine.

Led by the light of Faith serenely beaming,
With glowing hearts by His cradle we stand.
So led by light of a star sweetly gleaming,
Here come the wise men from the Orient land.
The King of Kings lay thus in lowly manger;
In all our trials born to be our friend.

He knows our need, to our weaknesses no stranger,
Behold your King! Before Him lowly bend!
Behold your King, Before Him lowly bend!

Truly He taught us to love one another;
His law is love and His gospel is peace.
Chains shall He break for the slave is our brother;
And in His name all oppression shall cease.
Sweet hymns of joy in grateful chorus raise we,
Let all within us praise His holy name.

Christ is the Lord! O praise His Name forever,
His power and glory evermore proclaim.
His power and glory evermore proclaim.

O Little Town of Bethlehem

18

O little town of Bethlehem,
How still we see thee lie!
Above thy deep and dreamless sleep
The silent stars go by;
Yet in thy dark streets shineth
The everlasting Light;
The hopes and fears of all the years
Are met in thee tonight.

For Christ is born of Mary,
And gathered all above,
While mortals sleep, the angels keep
Their watch of wondering love.
O morning stars, together
Proclaim the holy birth!
And praises sing to God the King,
And peace to men on earth.

How silently, how silently,
The wondrous gift is given!
So God imparts to human hearts
The blessings of his heaven.
No ear may hear his coming,
But in this world of sin,
Where meek souls will receive him, still
The dear Christ enters in.

Where children pure and happy
Pray to the blessed Child,
Where misery cries out to thee,
Son of the mother mild;
Where charity stands watching
And faith holds wide the door,
The dark night wakes, the glory breaks,
And Christmas comes once more.

O holy Child of Bethlehem!
Descend to us, we pray;
Cast out our sin and enter in,
Be born in us today.
We hear the Christmas angels
The great glad tidings tell;
O come to us, abide with us,
Our Lord Emmanuel!

SILENT NIGHT

19

Silent night, holy night,
All is calm, all is bright
Round yon virgin mother and child.
Holy infant, so tender and mild,
Sleep in heavenly peace,
Sleep in heavenly peace.

Silent night, holy night,
Shepherds quake at the sight;
Glories stream from heaven afar,
Heavenly hosts sing Alleluia!
Christ the Savior is born,
Christ the Savior is born!

Silent night, holy night,
Son of God, love's pure light;
Radiant beams from thy holy face
With the dawn of redeeming grace,
Jesus, Lord, at thy birth,
Jesus, Lord, at thy birth.

THE First Noel

20

The First Noel, the Angels did say
Was to certain poor shepherds in fields as they lay
In fields where they lay keeping their sheep
On a cold winter's night that was so deep.
Noel, Noel, Noel, Noel
Born is the King of Israel!

They looked up and saw a star
Shining in the East beyond them far
And to the earth it gave great light
And so it continued both day and night.
Noel, Noel, Noel, Noel
Born is the King of Israel!

And by the light of that same star
Three Wise men came from country far
To seek for a King was their intent
And to follow the star wherever it went.
Noel, Noel, Noel, Noel
Born is the King of Israel!

This star drew nigh to the northwest
O'er Bethlehem it took its rest
And there it did both pause and stay
Right o'er the place where Jesus lay.
Noel, Noel, Noel, Noel
Born is the King of Israel!

Then entered in those Wise men three
Fell reverently upon their knee
And offered there in His presence
Their gold and myrrh and frankincense.
Noel, Noel, Noel, Noel
Born is the King of Israel!

Then let us all with one accord
Sing praises to our heavenly Lord
That hath made Heaven and earth of nought
And with his blood mankind has bought.
Noel, Noel, Noel, Noel
Born is the King of Israel!

The Twelve Days of Christmas

21

On the first day of Christmas my true love sent to me
A partridge in a pear tree.

On the second day of Christmas my true love sent to me
Two turtle doves
And a partridge in a pear tree.

On the third day of Christmas my true love sent to me
Three French hens,
Two turtle doves,
And a partridge in a pear tree.

On the fourth day of Christmas my true love sent to me
Four calling birds,
Three French hens,
Two turtle doves,
And a partridge in a pear tree.

On the fifth day of Christmas my true love sent to me
Five gold rings
Four calling birds,
Three French hens,
Two turtle doves,
And a partridge in a pear tree.

(continued on next page)

On the sixth day of Christmas my true love sent to me
Six geese a-laying,
Five gold rings
Four calling birds,
Three French hens,
Two turtle doves,
And a partridge in a pear tree.

On the seventh day of Christmas my true love sent to me
Seven swans a-swimming,
Six geese a-laying,
Five gold rings
Four calling birds,
Three French hens,
Two turtle doves,
And a partridge in a pear tree.

On the eighth day of Christmas my true love sent to me
Eight maids a-milking,
Seven swans a-swimming,
Six geese a-laying,
Five gold rings
Four calling birds,
Three French hens,
Two turtle doves,
And a partridge in a pear tree.

On the ninth day of Christmas my true love sent to me
Nine ladies dancing,
Eight maids a-milking,
Seven swans a-swimming,
Six geese a-laying,
Five gold rings
Four calling birds,
Three French hens,
Two turtle doves,
And a partridge in a pear tree.

On the tenth day of Christmas my true love sent to me
Ten lords a-leaping,
Nine ladies dancing,
Eight maids a-milking,
Seven swans a-swimming,
Six geese a-laying,
Five gold rings
Four calling birds,
Three French hens,
Two turtle doves,
And a partridge in a pear tree.

On the eleventh day of Christmas my true love sent to me
Eleven pipers piping,
Ten lords a-leaping,
Nine ladies dancing,
Eight maids a-milking,
Seven swans a-swimming,
Six geese a-laying,
Five gold rings
Four calling birds,
Three French hens,
Two turtle doves,
And a partridge in a pear tree.

On the twelfth day of Christmas my true love sent to me
Twelve drummers drumming,
Eleven pipers piping,
Ten lords a-leaping,
Nine ladies dancing,
Eight maids a-milking,
Seven swans a-swimming,
Six geese a-laying,
Five gold rings
Four calling birds,
Three French hens,
Two turtle doves,
And a partridge in a pear tree.

UP ON THE HOUSETOP

22

Up on the housetop reindeer pause
Out jumps good old Santa Claus.
Down through the chimney, with lots of toys,
All for the little ones' Christmas joys.

CHORUS:
Ho, ho, ho! Who wouldn't go.
Ho, ho, ho! Who wouldn't go,
Up on the house top, click, click, click;
Down through the chimney with good Saint Nick.

First comes the stocking of little Nell;
Oh, dear Santa fill it well!
Give her a dolly that laughs and cries;
One that will open and shut her eyes.
(repeat chorus)

Next comes the stocking of little Will;
Oh just see what a glorious fill!
Here is a hammer and lots of tacks;
A whistle and a ball and a whip that cracks!
(repeat chorus)

WE Three Kings

23

We Three Kings of Orient are,
Bearing gifts we traverse afar,
Field and fountain,
Moor and mountain,
Following yonder Star.

CHORUS:
O Star of Wonder, Star of Night,
Star with Royal Beauty bright,
Westward leading,
Still proceeding,
Guide us to Thy perfect Light.

Born a King on Bethlehem plain,
Gold I bring to crown Him again,
King for ever,
Ceasing never
Over us all to reign.
(repeat chorus)

Frankincense to offer have I,
Incense owns a Deity nigh:
Prayer and praising
All men raising,
Worship Him God on High.
(repeat chorus)

Myrrh is mine; its bitter perfume
Breathes a life of gathering gloom;
Sorrowing, sighing,
Bleeding, dying,
Sealed in the stone-cold tomb.
(repeat chorus)

Glorious now behold Him arise,
King, and God, and Sacrifice;
Heav'n sings Hallelujah:
Hallelujah the earth replies.
(repeat chorus)

We Wish
You A Merry
Christmas

24

We wish you a merry Christmas,
We wish you a merry Christmas,
We wish you a merry Christmas
And a happy New Year.
Good tidings we bring
To you and your kin;
We wish you a merry Christmas
And a happy New Year!

Oh, bring us some figgy pudding,
Oh, bring us some figgy pudding,
Oh, bring us some figgy pudding,
And bring it right here.
Good tidings we bring
To you and your kin;
We wish you a merry Christmas
And a happy New Year!

We won't go till we get some,
We won't go till we get some,
We won't go till we get some,
So bring it right here.
Good tidings we bring
To you and your kin;
We wish you a merry Christmas
And a happy New Year!

We all like our figgy pudding,
We all like our figgy pudding,
We all like our figgy pudding,
With all its good cheers
Good tidings we bring
To you and your kin
We wish you a merry Christmas
And a happy New Year.

WHAT CHILD IS THIS?

25

What child is this, who, laid to rest,
On Mary's lap is sleeping?
Whom angels greet with anthems sweet,
While shepherds watch are keeping?

This, this is Christ the King,
Whom shepherds guard and angels sing:
Haste, haste to bring him laud,
The babe, the son of Mary.

So bring him incense, gold, and myrrh,
Come, peasant, king, to own him.
the King of kings salvation brings,
Let loving hearts enthrone him.

Raise, raise the song on high!
While Mary sings a lullaby.
Joy, joy for Christ is born,
The Babe, the son of Mary.

Holiday
Guest
Book

Thank You for joining us and for helping to make our Season Merry & Bright!

It's not what's under the tree,
it's who's gathered around it.

Guests

Name:..

Date:..

Comments:..

....

....

....

Name:..

Date:..

Comments:..

....

....

....

Name:..

Date:..

Comments:..

....

....

....

Guests

Name:

Date:

Comments:

Name:

Date:

Comments:

Name:

Date:

Comments:

Guests

Name:

Date:

Comments:

Name:

Date:

Comments:

Name:

Date:

Comments:

Guests

Name:..

Date:...

Comments:..

....

....

....

Name:..

Date:...

Comments:..

....

....

....

Name:..

Date:...

Comments:..

....

....

....

Guests

Name:

Date:

Comments:

Name:

Date:

Comments:

Name:

Date:

Comments:

Guests

Name:..

Date:...

Comments:...

....

....

....

HOLIDAY TRIVIA ANSWERS

Q. How many reindeer pull Santa's sleigh?
A: Eight

Q. How many times is figgy pudding demanded in the song, "We Wish You a Merry Christmas"?
A: Three

Q. What two reindeer names start with the letter "C"?
A: Cupid and Comet

Q. In the song, "The 12 Days of Christmas", what is given on the 9th day?
A: Nine ladies dancing

Q. In what year was the first Christmas tree erected at Rockefeller Center in New York City?
A: 1933

Q. What fabric was Frosty's hat made from?
A: Silk

Q. According to Clarence in the classic movie, *It's a Wonderful Life*, what happens every time a bell rings?
A: An angel gets its wings

Q. How many ghosts visit Scrooge in *A Christmas Carol* and what are their names?
A: Three ghosts by the names of Christmas Past, Present and Yet to Come

Q. In which Christmas carol do the names Little Nell and Little Will appear?
A: "Up on the Housetop"

Q. Which U.S. state was the first to recognize Christmas as a holiday?
A: Alabama, in 1836.

MERRY
Christmas
TO ALL!